George Paston

The Career of Candida

George Paston

The Career of Candida

ISBN/EAN: 9783337060381

Printed in Europe, USA, Canada, Australia, Japan

Cover: Foto ©ninafisch / pixelio.de

More available books at **www.hansebooks.com**

THE
CAREER OF CANDIDA

BY

GEORGE PASTON

AUTHOR OF
A MODERN AMAZON, A STUDY IN PREJUDICES, ETC.

"Only a learned and a manly soul
I purposed her, that should with even powers
The rock, the spindle, and the shears control
Of destiny, and spin her own free hours."
BEN JONSON

NEW YORK
D. APPLETON AND COMPANY
1897

Authorized Edition.

THE CAREER OF CANDIDA.

CHAPTER I.

THE St. John household, or rather the feminine part of it, was in a state of the deepest consternation and dismay, for the daughter and heiress of the house had refused to say her accustomed prayers. The rebel, aged eight, standing up straight and stiff in her little frilled nightgown, shook her curly mane, and obstinately refused to bow the knee.

"You naughty girl!" panted her mother, who had been summoned in haste from the drawing-room, and who was flushed with the reluctant irritation of a stout woman. "If you don't kneel down directly I shall have to fetch your father."

"Little 'gells that don't say their prayers when they are bid won't go to heaven," said the old nurse, who had washed and slapped her middle-aged mistress, and whose theology was that of an earlier generation.

By this time grandmamma and Aunt Agnes had arrived on the scene.

"You'll never get married when you grow up, my dear, if you don't say your prayers and go to church regularly," said old Mrs. St. John, who had been a beauty in her youth, and whose eyes, carriage, and complexion were still the envy and despair of younger generations. "Men prefer religious girls for their wives."

"And only think what Mr. Daintrey would say if he could see you now," put in Miss Agnes, pathetically. "He would be so very, very grieved."

Mr. Daintrey was the new curate.

"I don't care," said Candida, with another shake of her curls. "I don't want to marry anybody but papa, and he wouldn't refuse me, however naughty I was. And I don't care to go to heaven, because nurse says I can't have a pony there. And I shall be very glad if you will fetch papa, because he will understand."

So Mr. St. John's study was invaded by a distracted-looking female, and he, too, was bidden to the conclave.

"Well, what's all this about?" he inquired, as he entered the nursery, bringing, as the women felt, a judicial masculine mind to bear upon the difficulty which threatened to disturb the peace and blessedness of the house. "Why this sudden disbelief in the efficacy of prayer?"

"Will you listen to me if I tell you, without getting cross and saying how wicked I am?" asked his daughter. "Because I don't really mean to be wicked. I'm only trying not to be a whited sepulchre."

"I will listen with attention and toleration to all that you have to say," he replied gravely, "and reserve my own remarks till you have quite finished."

"Thank you," said Candida. "Well, I am not going to pray any more because I don't get what I pray for. The Bible says, 'Ask, and ye shall receive.' Now, I have prayed for things till I quite ached inside, but I never received them. I wanted a Newfoundland puppy, and I've prayed for him ever since before last Christmas, but he hasn't come. And I don't always pray for what I want myself. On your last birthday I heard you say at dessert that you had got up your last bottle of 'forty-seven port, and you wished you had another twenty dozen, so I prayed ever so hard that God would send you twenty dozen 'forty-seven port. I know I got the numbers right; but you said only yesterday that you should have to buy some new port, and wait till it was fit to drink."

"But the Bible means spiritual blessings when it says, 'Ask, and ye shall receive,'" put in Aunt Agnes, who was accustomed to talk as if she possessed a private key to the Scriptures.

"Well, I've prayed 'God bless father, and mother, and granny, and Aunt Aggy' ever since I was quite a little thing," answered her niece, more in sorrow than in anger, "and I can't see that you are any blesseder than you were when I began. Anyway, you're always saying you are miserable sinners."

"You can't tell how much less blessed we might all have been but for your petitions," said Mr. St. John, who had won his small daughter's confidence by always talking to her as if she were a reasonable being. "And I'll tell you what I should do, Candida. Instead of asking for new things, which there may be some excellent reason that you shouldn't have, I should pray that I might keep what I had got. There's poor old Boxer—he's a very good fellow, though he may not be equal to a Newfoundland pup; and there's the pony and your mother and me, to say nothing of your grandmother and aunt. I think you would be sorry to lose any of us, particularly the pony. So why not pray that we may all be preserved, and perhaps in the course of time a Newfoundland pup may be added unto you. I cannot say that I have much hope of the 'forty-seven port."

Candida considered for a moment. "Yes," she decided at length. "I don't mind doing that."

Without more ado she plumped down upon her knees, shut her eyes, folded her hands, and whispered her petitions in the orthodox attitude of an infant at prayer.

"Doesn't she look like a little angel, bless her?" murmured Aunt Agnes, the tears rising to her pale eyes. "'Out of the mouths of babes and sucklings——'"

"All the same," observed the little angel, suddenly scrambling to her feet, "I don't think the Bible ought to say, 'Ask, and ye shall receive,' if it doesn't really mean it."

It was mainly owing to her father's peculiar views and eccentric theories that Candida passed a very happy childhood.

"We have brought a girl-child into the world," he was accustomed to say, when his wife complained of the unusual character of their daughter's education. "Therein we have done her an irreparable injury. The only compensation that we can make her is to let her be a boy as long as possible."

So it came about that during the first sixteen years of our heroine's life she was attired in tunic and knickerbockers, had her hair cropped, was encouraged to climb trees and ride the pony astride and given, much against her will, a liberal education. Mr. Ferrars, the vicar, once a well-known university coach, instructed her in Latin, English, and mathematics, while her father taught her Greek. Candida only enjoyed her lessons with her father, but she worked splendidly for the vicar, because, being a confirmed woman-hater, he constantly expressed the opinion that it was no use trying to give a "female thing" a man's education, since she could have neither the intelligence nor the industry to profit by it. So when Candida was inclined to be idle or inattentive, her master's contemptuous, "How like a girl!" roused her energies like the prick of a spur. It was fortunate, perhaps, that she could not remember how when Ted Ferrars, the vicar's only son, played truant from his lessons to roam about the fields, his father only smiled indulgently, and said, "Boys will be boys."

But Ted was six or seven years older than Candida, and a great personage in her eyes, whom she could never have imagined guilty of fleeing from his books, since he had become a fine scholar as well as a distinguished athlete. She was only too proud when Ted would let her run about after him in the long vacation, and give her valuable instruction in tennis, cricket, or shooting at a mark.

When Candida could get neither her father nor Ted as a companion, she spent her spare time in the stable with Lester, the old coachman, or riding about the farms with Flaxman, the old bailiff. Nearly all the Branksmead servants were old. For girls she had at that time a supreme contempt, regarding them as inferior animals who were unable to throw straight, dreaded getting wet, and cried when they were hurt.

If Candida had a contempt for her own kind, it must be owned that she herself was a source of the deepest anxiety and misgiving to all her feminine relations. Her aunt and grandmother were constantly lamenting over the probable fate of the poor unfortunate child, who was growing up so rough and wild—a regular young hoyden. No man, they feared, would ever think of marrying her unless she changed her ways, took some interest in her appearance, learnt to play the piano, and paid more attention to needlework. It was such a pity they thought, that her father should have put the idea of working for a living into her head. They knew that the times were very bad, they were always having the agricultural depression dinned into their ears, but they were sure there would always be enough for them all to live upon. There could be no necessity that a Miss St. John, of Branksmead, should have to stoop so far as to work for her bread.

It was not until Candida was sixteen that Mrs. St. John, an easy-going woman by nature, was so far worked upon by her mother and sister-in-law as to rebel in some measure against her husband's system.

"How much longer do you intend to let Candida be a boy?" she asked him one day as they stood watching their daughter's efforts to "gentle" a particularly irritable young colt.

"Oh, I don't know," he answered uneasily, for there was a touch of sarcasm in her tone. "She seems very happy as she is. Why should we make any change till we are obliged? The miseries of young ladyhood will fall upon her quite soon enough."

"I think you ought to try and realize," said his wife, firmly, "that Candida is nearly grown-up, that she will soon be a woman. Nothing you can say or do will alter that fact. And the longer she goes on pretending to be a sort of boy, the more difficult she will find it to turn into a young lady."

There was reason in this, and Mr. St. John, though a man of theory, was able to see reason when it was put to him plainly.

"What do you wish me to do?" he asked.

"Begin by letting me put Candida into long skirts. Those short petticoats and knickerbockers look quite disgraceful on a girl of her size."

"But have you forgotten that picture of the Duchess of Strathpfeffer in her shooting-costume?" asked her husband. "Her skirts were quite as short as Candida's, and her figure not nearly so well adapted to knickerbockers.

That picture of the duchess had been his trump-card for the past year or two, but the duchess was to avail him no longer.

"I haven't forgotten," said Mrs. St. John; "but, of course, the duchess only wears that costume in the Highlands, where it would be quite in keeping. I don't object to Candida wearing her short skirts about the grounds, or even in the village, because people are used to seeing her dressed like that, and everybody knows that she is Miss St. John. But she ought to have proper clothes to wear when she drives out with me, and goes into Brancaster. And long skirts will help to tame her more than anything. She won't be able to ride bare-backed, or jump fences, or climb trees in them. They will be an education in nice, gentle, feminine ways."

"I accept the compromise under protest," said Mr. St. John. "If you women choose to think that nature's provision of two legs is indecent, and therefore handicap yourselves by pretending to move about on a draped pedestal, I suppose we have no right to complain. Such a proceeding throws all the prizes of life into our hands."

Thus it came about that a fashionable costume was ordered for Candida, who was invested with it in all state on her seventeenth birthday. With the long skirt and the tight-fitting bodice she acquired certain ideas and sensations which hitherto had been absent from her mind. For the first time she looked in the glass for another purpose than to see if her face was clean, twisted up her pig-tail into a tight knot at the back of her head, and held her breath in true feminine fashion when her waist measurement was taken. Though she had studied anatomy, it was something of a shock to her when the tape registered a full twenty-five inches. Truly, her initiation into the ways of young ladyhood had begun.

After breakfast came a serious conversation with her father in the study.

"You are nearly a woman," began the squire, "and it will soon be time for you to choose a profession. As you know, the estate, such as it is, goes to your cousin at my death, and your mother and aunt will be left with the very smallest income upon which they can live in any sort of comfort. Owing to the bad times through which all persons connected with the land are now passing, it is with the utmost difficulty that I can keep my head above water, and pay the interest on the mortgages. The truest kindness that I can show you is to give you a good training for any profession that you may fancy, and thus arm you to fight your own battle against the world, since every year will probably make it more and more impossible for me to assist you. You can understand that where the women of the past generations are helpless and entirely dependent upon their male relations, as in the case of your grandmother and aunt, it becomes necessary for the women of the present to work for themselves. It is no hardship, in my opinion, since, next to health, a congenial occupation is the first essential to human happiness. Have you come to any decision with regard to your future career?"

"I have been thinking about it for years," replied Candida. "Of course, I always knew that I was to work for my living. In fact, I couldn't have lived at home all my life doing nothing, like Aunt Aggie; it would have driven me melancholy mad. But the worst of it is that the things I should like best to do are supposed to be impracticable for a woman."

"Ah, I remember your telling me some time ago that you would like to be a veterinary surgeon. I think it probable that you might have practised that profession with very good success, but, unfortunately, it is closed to ladies. Have you no other ideas?"

"I used to think I should like to go out to America and lasso mustangs on the prairies, as they do in boys' books; but, of course, that was only a childish fancy. I should have been quite satisfied to read for the Bar, like Ted; but that door is shut in my face. I should like a little more time in which to make up my mind."

"Very well," said her father. "There is no hurry. If no better plan presents itself, you shall go to Girton for three years, at the end of which time, if you have worked well, various occupations will be open to you. I see Ted Ferrars coming up the drive. Tell him to stop to luncheon, and take you for a walk afterwards."

CHAPTER II.

THE fact that Ted Ferrars seemed considerably impressed by the long skirts and grown-up air of his girl friend, afforded Candida not a little pride and gratification. For the first time in their acquaintance he treated her with the somewhat formal and distant courtesy which he considered the proper attitude towards a full-fledged young lady. Ted was not much accustomed to feminine society, and blissfully ignorant of the ways of women. He had no sisters, and could not remember his mother; consequently, as his father sometimes observed, he thought that all women were angels. Hitherto, he had regarded Candida as a nice little fellow of no particular sex, and it was rather a shock to him, on coming home after six months' absence, to find that she had developed into a creature whom he instinctively took off his hat to, and allowed to pass through a door in front of him.

By the time they had tramped a couple of miles together, however, the strangeness had worn off, and he was descanting at great length and with overwhelming fluency upon his literary idol of the hour, Matthew Arnold. Ted was at the somewhat trying age when a new mental phase is gone through about once in three months, the malady, for such it is, varying in duration and intensity with the power and fascination of the author under whose influence the patient has temporarily fallen. When Ted was thoroughly interested in a man or book, he would pour out his mind on the subject to any one who would listen, or even pretend to listen, to him. He preferred a sympathetic audience, but he would discourse to a post rather than keep his valuable ideas to himself. Candida listened rather inattentively as he declaimed the doctrines of sweetness and light, but she inwardly wondered how a man who had rowed stroke in his college boat, and was the best swift bowler in the county cricket-club, could be so enthusiastic about any book or writer. In her eyes the trail of "lessons" still hung about all books, and authors she regarded as unnecessarily tiresome, long-winded persons.

Another reason for her inattention lay in the fact that the roads were muddy, and that it was necessary for her to hold up her skirt, which wound itself round her legs in a particularly exasperating manner, and made their four-miles-an-hour pace an unusual strain upon her powers.

"Well, but what does Arnold want us to do?" she

asked at length, getting rather tired of the reiteration of such phrases as "conduct is three-fourths of life," "the Eternal not ourselves," "sweet reasonableness," and so forth.

"Well, we must control our natural impulses of self-preservation and re———" Ted pulled himself up short in his glib citation. "Oh, you wouldn't understand that yet. And we must get culture; that is, get to know the best that has been said and written upon every subject. Otherwise we shall only be barbarians or Philistines. But, above all, Candida"—and here his eager, ugly face glowed with enthusiasm—"we must try to be a remnant."

"A what?" asked Candida, a faint reminiscence of a shopping excursion during the summer sales floating through her mind.

"A remnant. You see, the elect always constitute a small remnant of a nation, just as they did with the Jews and Greeks. The great mass of the people are ignorant, sordid, blown about with every wind. They are the mob, the rabble who cry 'Hosanna!' one day and 'Crucify him!' the next."

"In that case," said Candida, thoughtfully, "we ought to be governed by a minority. How funny it would be if the candidates at an election each wanted to come in at the bottom of the poll, and tried to persuade their voters to plump for their rivals. It would be a sort of political donkey-race. Oh, don't look so cross, Ted; I'm afraid I shall never be a remnant. Shall we take the short cut home through the meadows? I have made my arm ache holding up my skirt."

The pair turned into a by-lane which led to the gate of the water-meadows. It was a six-barred gate, and it was locked. Ted vaulted lightly over, and Candida was about to do the same, when she remembered her new attire.

"Bother this skirt!" she grumbled, as she climbed bar by bar to the top of the gate. Rejecting Ted's proffered hand, she attempted to jump down, but her skirt catching on a projecting piece of wood, she fell to the ground with a force which made her nose bleed, and flashed stars before her eyes. It was a new and most humiliating experience, for though she had often met with accidents before, they had hitherto been unavoidable, the result of some piece of hardihood on her own part. But she had never fallen off an ordinary gate in that helpless feminine fashion, and she felt thoroughly degraded in her own sight.

Much to Ted's surprise and consternation, his companion, instead of jumping up and laughing at her own clumsiness, sat still upon the muddy ground, and burst into tears.

"Oh, I'm afraid you have hurt yourself badly," said the young man, kneeling down beside her. "Do you think you have broken any bones? Shall I run and fetch you some water?"

"No, no," wept Candida. "I'm not hurt—not to matter. It's all this beastly skirt. I shall never, never be happy again. I can't even jump off a gate."

"Oh, well, never mind," said Ted, awkwardly, as he tried to wipe off the mud from her face with his pocket-handkerchief. "It's what all girls have to put up with, you know, so I suppose it's all right. And you'll get used to it in no time, I expect."

"It's not all right," cried Candida, passionately; "it's perfectly infernal, and I shall never get used to it, not if I live to be a hundred. Father was right when he said this morning that I was being crippled for life. But please go away and leave me alone, Ted. I hate to be pitied; I prefer to be miserable all by myself."

Thus bidden, Ted went reluctantly away. If he himself had fallen into such a plight, he knew that he should have much preferred no eye-witness of his woe. Yet there seemed something horribly unchivalrous in leaving a lady to sit on the ground and mingle her tears with her blood. He compromised the matter by hiding behind a tree at a respectful distance, until he saw the disconsolate damsel rise to her feet, go and wash her face in the brook that flowed through the meadow, and then set off towards home.

On arriving at the Hall, Candida went straight to the study, where she found the squire busy over his accounts.

"Father," she said in the tone of one who has just taken a solemn resolution, "I have quite made up my mind about my future profession. I wish to be an acrobat."

"An acrobat!" said Mr. St. John, raising his eyebrows in mild surprise. "Isn't this a little sudden? May I ask what has led you to this decision?"

"Acrobats don't wear skirts," returned Candida, promptly. "It is the only profession I can think of, the practice of which will ensure me the free use of my limbs."

"I'm afraid that acrobats have to begin their training in the nursery," said Mr. St. John. "And I fancy they are usually chosen from among those who have an hereditary gift for tumbling, which is not the case with you. But there are so many new occupations for women nowadays that there may be another which would meet your requirements. I will write to my old friend, Mrs. Festus, and ask her advice. She combines all the experience of age with much of the liberality and enlightenment of youth."

"Thank you," said Candida, carefully feeling her nose, which seemed to be gradually increasing in size and heat. "If anything could reconcile me to being a girl it would be having a man like you for my father. You never seem to think that because I am thirty years younger than you I must be thirty times more foolish."

Candida's appearance, and the accident that had

damaged her beauty, called forth a good deal of comment at the afternoon tea-table.

"A young lady of seventeen," said her mother, "should know better than to go careering across country, and climbing over gates. Why can't you walk quietly through the lanes as your aunts and I used to do when we were girls? If we came to a stile or a locked gate we turned back at once; we had too much consideration for our frocks to risk soiling or tearing them. Your new dress is covered with mud, and torn out at the gathers."

"We used to walk in the fields sometimes when I was a girl, but only if we had a gentleman to escort us," put in Miss Agnes, gently. "I remember one day we were out with Sir James Courthope, and we met a dreadful cow which we thought was a mad bull. I fainted dead away, and my sister Ellen nearly went into hysterics, and Sir James had to fetch a carriage to take us home."

"You seem to have given a great deal of unnecessary trouble," remarked Candida. "Poor Sir James!"

"Men prefer women who are timid and helpless," said the dowager Mrs. St. John, who always spoke of men with the air of one having authority. "And let me tell you, Candida, they don't admire young ladies with scratched hands and swollen noses. You will never be a social success if you don't alter your ways very much. When I was your age I was engaged in my third love affair and by the time I was eighteen I had had nineteen proposals. Did I ever tell you about the first time I went to the opera, and how the young queen, who was then a bride, was deeply annoyed because the princes and the gentlemen of the royal party did nothing but stare at our box?"

"That was certainly very ill-mannered," said Candida, gravely. She had heard the anecdote many times before, and was aware that her comment was not exactly of the kind that was expected or desired.

In the course of two or three days Mrs. Festus's reply to her old friend's letter arrived. The acrobatic idea she dismissed at once as out of the question. "But," she proceeded, "if your daughter wishes for an active career, her best plan would be to go into training as a gymnastic-instructor. The profession is not as yet overcrowded, few ladies having taken it up, while there are new openings in connection with high schools and colleges every year. The training, which lasts about two years, should begin when a girl is seventeen or eighteen years of age, and at the end of the second year, if she has made the most of her time, she should have little difficulty in obtaining an appointment. I understand that well-qualified, experienced teachers who have taken up musical drill, fencing, and skirt-dancing, as well as gymnastics proper, are able to earn two hundred a year and upwards at their profession. The fees amount to about thirty pounds a year, and I suppose there would be a premium; but I can obtain all particulars from my friend, Miss Mason, the head of the Bloomsbury Gymnasium for Women.

"If your Candida takes to the idea, let her come to me for the time of her training. She would have two young companions in my house, one studying painting and the other medicine."

Candida did take to the idea very eagerly, for work which consisted chiefly of climbing, jumping, vaulting and swinging sounded like the most delightful kind of play. Latterly her athletic feats had been performed in secret with the consciousness that should they come to her mother's ears they would be looked upon with disapproval as unseemly for a young lady of seventeen. But now those restless limbs and active muscles of hers would be allowed full scope, and the performances which had hitherto been regarded as hoydenish, would be smiled upon as praiseworthy efforts to improve herself in her profession. Some opposition the new plan met with from the feminine part of the family, for though they had but the vaguest ideas about the calling of gymnastic instructor, the novelty of the occupation made them suspect that it must be eccentric, and unsuited to the dignity of a Miss St. John of Branksmead, even though Branksmead were a falling house. But the squire was firm in his determination that his daughter should be as free to choose her own vocation in life as though she were his son.

So it came about that one morning early in October, Candida, outwardly cheerful and of good courage, but inwardly shivering and forlorn, set out alone upon her first flight into the strange world. Her father had insisted that she should be unsupported on this occasion by either her mother or himself. The sooner she learnt independence and self-reliance the better, he declared; and besides, young people always got on better with strangers, and were less inclined to be self-conscious when deprived of the countenance of their nearest relatives. The following letter was received at Branksmead on the day but one after her departure:—

"200, Bloomsbury Square,
" October 8th, 188-.

"MY DEAR FATHER AND MOTHER,

"You will have got my telegram yesterday saying that I arrived safely in Bloomsbury Square. It seems a long time ago already; so much has happened since. I think I shall like Mrs. Festus, though she is rather alarming at first sight, being so big and handsome, and having such very white hair, with such piercing dark eyes. She is quite different from any other woman I have ever known; I mean in her ideas and opinions. She told me she had only one rule for her household, and that was ' Live and let live.' She says that most women martyrize themselves and everybody about them with fussy little rules, which are more honoured in the breach than the observance. She thinks, after studying my face, that my imagination and emotional nature have not been sufficiently cultivated, and she is going to put me through a course of novels and poetry. She told me, also, to talk to the servants, and try to get upon confidential terms with them. Isn't that funny? She brought in the tea herself because the parlour-maid was having a violin lesson.

"At dinner I saw the other girls who are living here. The medical one is plain, and has a bumpy forehead. The artist one would be pretty if her hair were not like a deserted bird's-nest, and if she did not wear such queer clothes. I like her the best, though. She said she hoped I was not intellectual, as she was tired of being the only fool in the house. About half an hour after dinner the three maids came into the drawing-room, and Mrs. Festus read aloud out of a book called "Christie Johnstone." The cook, who is rather stout, groaned at intervals, but Mrs. Festus said afterwards that she always groans at the passages she likes best. She says Mariana (that's the cook's name) is passionately fond of poetry, particularly of the morbid kind, but that she very seldom allows her to read any now because it makes her cry so that all the dishes are too salt.

"This morning Mrs. Festus went with me to the

Gymnasium, which is only five minutes' walk from here. Miss Mason, the chief, is a very clever woman; she can pull up on the bar with one hand. We did musical drill first, and afterwards exercises on the horizontal and parallel bars, the ladders, flying rings and vaulting-horse, as well as rope-climbing and the high jump. I was so stupid at everything except the vaulting and jumping that I felt horrribly ashamed of myself, but they were all very kind, and said I should be sure to get on because I was not afraid of falling about and hurting myself.

"I am going to be tremendously busy now, because there are several classes every day, and I have to attend anatomy lectures as well.

"Love to granny and Aunt Aggie.
  "Your affectionate daughter,
    "CANDIDA ST. JOHN."

CHAPTER III.

ON a July morning, two years later, Candida awoke to the delightful consciousness that she was free at last from a state of pupilage, having triumphantly passed all her examinations, and that as soon as the holidays were over the post awaited her of assistant instructor at the Bloomsbury Gymnasium, at a salary of sixty pounds a year. Meanwhile, it was pleasant to think of Branksmead, where she would be before the evening, and the two months' holidays, which had been well-earned by the past half-year of hard work, mental as well as physical. Her mind, which up to her eighteenth year had been far less developed than her body, had since begun to work with a vigour that bade fair to make up very quickly for its past inertia. A course of novels and poetry, as prescribed by Mrs. Festus, had roused her imagination and awakened in her a taste for reading for its own sake. In her spare time she greedily devoured books on any and every subject—history, science, philosophy ; nothing came amiss to her, and it was probably chiefly due to the excellence of her physical condition that she escaped a bad attack of mental indigestion. But when the brain is overloaded or over-stimulated, nothing can be better adapted to restore its equilibrium than for its owner to turn somersaults on the trapeze, or to "circle" round the horizontal bar until she can scarcely distinguish her heels from her head.

At nineteen, Candida had reached her full height of five feet nine, and she turned the scale at ten stone. In certain branches of her chosen profession she had gained considerable distinction, notably in those which required strength and nerve rather than grace or dexterity. She was an accomplished performer upon the horizontal and parallel bars, the vaulting-horse and swings. Her fencing was dashing and fearless, but rather lacking in neatness, while at skirt-dancing she was never more than a mediocre performer. Thanks to her good temper and genuine enthusiasm for her work, she had got on well with both pupils and instructors, and gave promise of herself becoming a successful teacher. In the course of her two years' training she had made several friends, but had remained entirely free from the interruptions or distractions of a love-affair, or even of a mild flirtation. Her observation had led her to the conclusion that love was trying to the temper and disastrous to the nerves, and consequently she had early made up her mind to keep clear of the tender passion, at any rate until she had gained a firm footing in her profession.

At Branksmead station the old coachman who had given her her first riding-lesson was waiting with the old dog-cart and the well-bred little mare which, in her shabby harness, looked like some fine lady masquerading in beggar's costume.

"Nancy looks very fit," remarked Candida, as they went swinging up the long hill from the station. "You haven't forgotten the old recipe for grooming a horse, I see, Lester."

"No, Miss Candy, no," replied the old man, with a chuckle. "The young fellows, they're mighty particular about their tools, and run their masters up a bill for more brushes and things than I know the names of, but they forget the elbow-grease—they forget the elbow-grease. They come a-driving over to the Hall, and turn up their noses at my harness-room, and think a lot of theirselves because they sit behind a dirty pair of jobbed horses. But I says I'd rather drive one beast as can hold up her head for herself, than two as have to have theirn strapped up with bearing-reins. And I takes my hand and rubs their hosses' coats the wrong way, and lawk! you should see the muck that comes out. Then I tells 'em they can stroke my mare any time with a fresh pipe-clayed glove, and no damage done. I don't groom her as if I was wiping a baby."

Candida laughed.

"I see the cart is getting the worse for wear," she said. "I suppose my father cannot afford to buy a new one, with two more farms thrown on his hands, and a further reduction of rents."

"No, no," grumbled the old man; "when the tenants want to live like fighting-cocks, the landlords have to pinch. These new-fangled farmers, with their hunters and pony-carriages and pianos, how do they think they're going to pay for all that off the land? Why, they don't get their breakfasts till near dinner-time, nor their dinners till bed-time. And their fine lady wives and daughters never go near the cows or the poultry. 'Nasty, dirty things!' they says. 'Oh no, I don't know the price of butter nor eggs. You must ask the dairy-woman or the hen-wife.' Now, you know, Miss Candy, the land won't stand that in good times, much less in bad."

They had now reached the lodge gates, and were soon spinning up the avenue that led to the Hall. Mr. St. John was standing on the steps to receive his daughter. She fancied that he looked greyer and more stooping than when she had last seen him only six months before.

"Poor father!" she said to herself, "I wish I could earn enough to help him. But, at least, I'll never be another burden to weigh him down."

The ladies of the family were assembled in the drawing-room, eagerly awaiting both the traveller and their tea, which they had postponed drinking until her arrival.

"Well, my child," said Mrs. St. John, standing on tip-toe to kiss her tall daughter. "Are you very tired after your long journey? You must be dying for your tea."

"Tired!" said Candida, in surprise. "Why, I've done nothing but sit perfectly still for the last three or four hours. I feel as fresh as a daisy. And I gave up tea some time ago; I find that my hand is steadier without it. No, no muffin, thank you; I should like some bread and butter, stale bread, please, and cut rather thick."

"Turn to the light, child, and let me see how you are looking," said her grandmother. "H'm, you have grown up to your features, and your complexion is clearer. But people will not climb on chairs to look at you, as they used to do at me. Did I ever tell you about the first time I went to the opera, and how annoyed the queen was because the princes did nothing but stare at our box?"

"I have no doubt you were well worth looking at," said Candida, who had learnt a little tolerance in the past two years. "As for me, I know I'm not a beauty, but I had better biceps than any other girl at the Gymnasium."

"Biceps! The idea of a young lady having biceps!" Mrs. St. John closed her eyes for a moment, as though to shut out the thought, then went on querulously, "It seems to me that the young people grow plainer and more unattractive every day. The new curate came to see me this morning, and you never saw such a nose as he has. It isn't a feature, it's a limb. A man with a nose like that ought never to have been ordained."

"Bishops evidently think that beauty is a snare," said her son, lightly. "You used to say that the last curate had a mouth like an earthquake."

"So he had," retorted the old lady. "And he made it worse by preaching two extempore sermons every Sunday."

"I should like to go out and look round the place before dinner," said Candida, who had disposed of her bread and butter. "Will you come, father?"

The pair went out together, the one young and supple and straight as an arrow, the other prematurely aged, bowed beneath the burden of a hopelessly encumbered estate and three helpless women. They went first to the stables, which presented a long row of loose boxes, all empty save for the one occupied by Nancy, who thrust her nose through the boxes in the well-founded expectation of sugar. The kennels were visited next, where dwelt in solitary grandeur an old setter, who showed but a chastened pleasure at the sight of his young mistress. Being a dog of conservative views, he could only feel a qualified approval of a young lady who was so ill-advised as to leave her home and family for ten months out of the twelve.

"We will talk over your plans for the future to-morrow morning," said her father. "This first evening shall be given up to frivolity. By the way, I suppose you know that Ted Ferrars is at home now? He is coming up some time to-morrow to see his old playfellow."

"I am very glad," said Candida. "I haven't seen Ted for months. He has been very busy, I believe, since he was called to the Bar; he seems to have made a good start in his profession."

* * * * * *

"That's not a bad tea-gown," observed Mrs. St. John the elder, looking critically at her granddaughter, as the four ladies sat together after dinner. "But I prefer to see young women in evening dress."

"I never wear evening dress," replied Candida.

"Yet you have such beautiful arms and shoulders," sighed her mother. "It seems a pity that nobody should ever see them."

"I suppose my husband will see them some day," said her daughter. "I don't consider that anybody else has any right to see them."

Miss Agnes blushed. She thought the conversation had taken an indelicate turn, which was somewhat inconsistent, considering that her own collar-bones were liberally displayed.

"Your husband!" repeated the dowager. "Have you ever had an offer of marriage?"

"No, not a ghost of one," replied Candida, cheerfully.

"And you are nineteen," said the old lady, reproachfully. "At your age I was married, and my husband was my twenty-fifth lover. But I suppose you modern young ladies despise men and marriage."

"Not at all. I consider that every healthy woman should be married by the time she is twenty-five, and a mother before she is thirty."

"My dear, what dreadful things you say," cried the three ladies, while Miss Agnes glanced at the door, as though meditating flight.

"Why?" asked Candida. "Is there anything dreadful in discussing some of the most important questions of life with the women of one's own family? I have every intention of marrying if I meet the right man, and I hope to justify my existence by carrying on the race as well as working for it."

"But supposing," hesitated her aunt, who was getting a little hardened to these continual shocks to her sense of propriety—"supposing you became attached to a gentleman who did not return your affection?"

Candida considered for a moment.

"Well, in that case," she replied at length, "I should have had a very valuable experience."

Mr. St. John, who had come into the room just as the last question was put, broke into a laugh.

"You are really very amusing, Candida," he said. "What a pity it is that you are quite unable to appreciate your own humour."

The next morning a prolonged discussion was held on the subject of ways and means, and plans for the future. Candida submitted to her parents' approval a scheme for sharing a lodging with her friend Sabina Romney, who had been a fellow-inmate with her of the house in Bloomsbury Square, and who had lately obtained an engagement at the Piccadilly Theatre, at the magnificent salary of three guineas a week.

"Sabina has some furniture that belonged to her mother," explained Candida. "So we think of taking three little unfurnished rooms somewhere near the Museum."

"And how will you pay your share of the board and lodging, and clothe yourself out of three and twenty shillings a week?" asked her father.

"Oh, it can be done," said his daughter, confidently. "There are lots of respectable women living in London on less than sixty pounds a year. I must have enough to eat, of course, but I shall make up my mind to go into no kind of society where dress matters, and as I shall be wearing my gymnasium costume for about eight hours a day, I shall want to buy very little, except boots. Then I have the promise of some private pupils, and after the summer holidays my salary is to be raised. I have thought it all out, and I am sure that I can manage with care and economy."

"Well," said her father, "if you can fight your way to success alone and unaided, so much the better. A touch of privation will do you no harm, and some day you will probably look back upon this period of struggle as the happiest time in your life. All the same, I shall pay a small sum into your account at the bank, which you can draw upon should you be ill or out of work."

"Ill!" cried Candida, squaring her shoulders. "Do I look as if I were likely to be ill? And as for the probability of being out of work—well, you haven't seen my certificates yet."

"And this Miss Romney," asked Mrs. St. John. "Is she a sensible sort of girl?"

"Well no," replied her daughter. "I don't think her worst enemy could call Sabina a sensible girl. She is very pretty and fascinating, and perfectly easy to get on with as long as she is not jealous of you, and she is never jealous of me. She is apt to fancy herself in love with some man or other, but it doesn't really mean anything, and she gets tired of them as soon as they fall in love with her. I know the worst of Sabina, and as I shall be out all day and she will be out all the evening, it will be strange if we can't manage to get on together."

"Well, it all seems very odd and peculiar," sighed

Mrs. St. John. "I suppose you'll never have proper meals, and you'll sit up late, and get your feet wet, and everybody will wonder what we can be thinking of to let you go and live in lodgings like a bachelor. However, I wash my hands of it all."

"Would you rather I spent my time like Aunt Aggie, in making comforters that nobody wears, and taking soup to people who throw it out of the window as soon as her back is turned?"

"No, but I should like you to go to parties and balls, and have pretty frocks, and get married, as I did when I was a girl."

"Unfortunately, nobody ever gives balls in this neighbourhood, and there are no men to marry, except poor Ted. And that reminds me, Ted is coming to have some singles with me to-day. I must go and cut the grass."

When Ted arrived he found his old playfellow engaged in running a good-sized lawn-mower over the grass.

"You can take the handles and steer," she said, in response to his offer of help. She harnessed herself to the ropes, and began to stride up and down at a pace that left her companion no inclination for speech.

"There, that has taken exactly thirty-five minutes," observed Candida, when the task was ended. "The gardener and the boy seldom do it under two hours. I took the place of the boy once, but the gardener broke down before we had cut half, and had to be restored with porter, so I thought I had better do it alone to-day. You look rather warm."

Ted, conscious of a scarlet face and streaming brow, murmured something apologetic about being out of training.

"We'll have some hard singles after lunch," said Candida. "That will soon get you into condition again."

He looked at her with surprise and a half unwilling admiration as she stood facing him, her breathing scarcely quickened, her cool cheek just tinged with pink. She had improved in appearance, he decided, during the four or five months that had elapsed since he had last seen her. She stood within an inch of his own height, and her figure, which, but for the culture it had received, might have been rather heavy for her age, was admirably lithe and supple. Her alert, fearless bearing, and the long sweeping line of her limbs recalled the classical enthusiasms of his college days, and he mentally compared her with some huntress nymph, swiftest-footed of the followers of Artemis. In face she was not, as her grandmother had remarked, a striking beauty. Abundant fair hair, clear blue-grey eyes, perfect teeth and an unimpeachable complexion were her chief attractions, for the mouth was too large and the line of jaw slightly too heavy, while there was as yet no subtlety in her expression, no challenge in her glance.

Ted wondered whether she had grown in mind as well as in body, and smiled involuntarily as he remembered his boyish outpourings into her unsympathetic ears. The same recollection recurred later to Candida herself, for while they were resting after a couple of hard singles she inquired—

"Who are the objects of your idolatry just now, Ted? The last time I saw you they were Ibsen and Tolstoi, and years ago I remember you at the Matthew Arnold stage. I have been through it all myself since then, even to the yearning to be a remnant.

"Then you find time to read?" he asked.

"Of course. Mrs. Festus says it is as foolish to say we have no time to read as it would be to say we have no time to eat. It was impossible to live with her and not get a taste for reading. Books were like live creatures to her; in fact, I am not sure that she does not love them better than human beings."

"I am glad she has infected you with her taste," said Ted. "One so seldom comes across a girl to whom one can talk about the books or subjects that really interest one, and yet I have often thought that it should be instructive to get at the feminine point of view. But, as a rule, if you discuss abstract topics with a girl you run the risk of either boring or shocking her."

"My experience is that men will seldom condescend to talk to girls as if they were reasonable beings," said

Candida. "You and I must set the rest of the world a better example, Ted. Tell me about your latest craze."

"It's not for remnants," he answered laughing. "Rather the other way. I've been tending towards socialism lately. Evolutionary socialism you understand," he added, with evident pride in the phrase.

"My mind is still in a fluid state on that and one or two other subjects," said Candida. "Of course, if I only studied one side of a question, after the most approved feminine fashion, I should find it easy enough to crystallize my ideas. But I must hear the evidence on both sides before I give a verdict."

The two solemn young faces drew nearer together, the two important young voices joined in a harmonious duet, as the couple exchanged threadbare phrases, and threshed out the empty husks of questions that had vainly vexed the minds of their grandfathers. Aunt Aggie, coming to call them into tea, a romantic interest in the young couple already stirring her tender heart, was chilled and disappointed to find them exchanging confidences on such subjects as land-tenure, nationalization of property, and industrial co-operation.

CHAPTER IV.

On the first Sunday after Candida's home-coming the household was shaken to its foundations by her announcement that she was not going to church. "This, then," cried the ladies of the family, "this was what came of educating a girl like a boy, allowing her to enter a profession, and bringing her up in ideas of independence; she turns out a free-thinker, an infidel, an atheist."

"Milton says," observed Candida, whose conscious integrity enabled her to remain calm in the midst of the agitation, "that if a man has no reason for the faith that is in him beyond the fact that it is taught him by his pastor and professed by his community, then his faith, however true, is for him heresy. In that sense I have been a heretic all my life. I had no right to form an opinion about any religion until I knew the arguments that could be urged against as well as for it. If I were the Creator, I should not be satisfied with a worship that was founded on wilful ignorance; I should regard it as an insult from the creatures upon whom I had bestowed the gift of reason."

"But what will the vicar think?" cried her mother, as though that were a far more important matter. "And the poor people—such a shocking example for them."

"Would you have me play a dishonest part in order that the poor people may be edified?" demanded Candida, with solemnity.

"I can't argue about it," said her mother, almost in tears. "I only know that it is very wrong, and—and unwomanly."

"If only you would have a little talk with Mr. Oriel," put in Miss Agnes, timidly, "I am sure he would smooth away all your difficulties."

"Come," said Mr. St. John, "it is time for us to start. Candida, we will leave you to prosecute your search for truth. There is a very complete edition of the Fathers in the library."

"Thank you," she replied. "At present I am studying the argument from design. I shall go for a walk in the fields."

"Don't take this phase too seriously," said the squire to his wife and sister, as they obeyed the summons of the bells. "It was bound to come sooner or later. I admit that our dear Candida is a bit of a prig at the present moment but then all properly brought up boys and girls are prigs at nineteen."

"It is not only her refusal to attend church that troubles me," said Mrs. St. John; "but she seems to have picked up such queer ideas from Mrs. Festus. She has been asking the poor women not to curtsey to her; she says she can't stand being bobbed to by her elders and betters. And the other day, when Jane was turning out her room, just because she fancied the girl looked pale and breathless, she sent her to lie down and did the room herself, scrubbing the floor and all. And she made me write to the stores for some very expensive iron medicine for Jane, who, she says, is anæmic. As if all young servants were not anæmic! It is really too upsetting."

Mr. St. John laughed.

"I believe Candida is perfectly right," he said. "Young people generally are right theoretically, only they are in too great a hurry to put their theories into practice. They are not content to grind slowly, though they are anxious to grind exceeding small. We elderly people are only useful as drags upon the wheels of their splendid energy. If it were not for us they would turn the world upside down once a week and scrub it all over, entirely for its own good."

Meanwhile Candida had unchained the dog, and together they wandered through the fields, from which the last load of hay had been carried only the evening before. In a meadow that bounded the Vicarage glebe, she came upon Ted lying on his back beneath the shade of an elm, enjoying his morning pipe. He felt a slight shock of disapproval on seeing Candida. A man may be an honest doubter, but a woman! Surely she should cling to "her early heaven, her happier views."

"You have given up going to church," he said, as he sprang to his feet, and leaned over the gate by her side.

"For the present," she replied. "I am an inquirer."

"Ah," said Ted. "Men mostly pass through that phase at college. Some of them remain in it. What have you been bothering your head with? Kant, Schopenhauer, Herbert Spencer?"

"No," she confessed. "I can understand a plain fact in plain English, but metaphysics are beyond me. I have been reading history chiefly, and some physical science. It makes one feel very small to be brought face to face with the great facts of the universe. I feel sometimes as if I had lost a father, and been turned out of a comfortable home to wander in the desert. Yet the air of the desert is more bracing than that of the home, and the sense of space brings a sense of freedom."

"I know, I know," cried Ted, to whom the word "universe" was as the sound of the trumpet to a war-horse. "And the possibility that you may be alone, uncared-for, unregarded, an infinitesimal insect clinging for a few moments to the wheel of life, makes you feel only the more determined to play your little part as well as you can, and look facts in the face without whimpering."

The universe is always a fruitful, fascinating topic to young minds; it is also a safe one, for who could wax sentimental over such subjects as time, space, or eternity? The pair spent their Sunday morning most enjoyably in discussing problems that have perplexed the world since our ancestors lost their tails, abandoned their arboreal habits, and developed self-consciousness. Whence do we come? whither are we going? what are life, death, truth? These, and other hoary-headed questions they asked, and, unlike jesting Pilate, they waited for a reply. They were so young, they lived in such quickly moving times, that any morning they might wake to find that one of the riddles had been solved, or the veil of a great mystery rent in twain.

Ted quite forgot his disapproval of feminine freedom of thought in his enjoyment of the conversation. He knew very well what other young men of his own standing said and thought upon most of these subjects, but to discuss them with a woman was quite a different thing. The experience was piquant, instructive, stimulating; there were unexpected variations, digressions, disagreements; at any moment a gleam of light might be flashed upon a dark corner, or a fresh point of view disclosed. It was a great pity, he reflected, that men and women could not always be comrades, fellow-students of nature, co-seekers after truth. Yet it is to be doubted whether, if Candida's figure had been stumpy, her skin sallow, and her eyes spectacled, Ted would have found the conversation so supremely interesting. It is more than probable that he would have preferred his solitary pipe, and his undisturbed contemplation of the sky through the elm branches.

The following day Sabina Romney was expected at the Hall, where she had been invited to spend the remainder of the holidays.

"It has just occurred to me that we know nothing about your friend Sabina except that she is pretty and susceptible," observed Mr. St. John at breakfast. "Enlighten us, Candida. Has she any skeletons whose cupboards we must be careful to avoid? Who is she when she is not at the Piccadilly Theatre, and what are her people?"

"I don't think she has any people," replied Candida. "Her mother is dead, and she never had any real father."

"How did she manage that?"

"Well, her father was one of those people who think marriage immoral, and he converted her mother to his own belief in the virtuousness of a free union. They lived together till Sabina was about five years old, and then Mr. Romney fell in love with another woman. From his point of view, it then became sinful for him to go on living with Mrs. Romney, but, unfortunately, he could not afford to support more than one wife and family. He offered to provide for Sabina if her mother would give her up, but of course she refused. He ended by marrying the other woman, whom he could not convert to his own views, and wife number one slowly did herself to death with fine needlework. When Sabina was about sixteen she got a 'walk-on' at a theatre, and she has supported herself ever since. Her mother died about a year ago, and then she came to live with Mrs. Festus."

"A very instructive little story," remarked Mr. St. John. "Unfortunately for its professors, free love is a very expensive custom."

"Then this girl has no right to her name," said Mrs. St. John, in disapproving tones. "I don't think she is at all a nice friend for you, and I wonder Mrs. Festus took her into her house."

"It was her father's name," said Candida. "And it wasn't her fault that he was a selfish brute and her mother a weak fool. A girl can't choose her own parents, nor settle under what conditions she is to come into the world."

When Sabina arrived, it became clear that she would very soon make her peace with offended propriety in the person of Mrs. St. John. She was an exceedingly pretty girl, with appealing brown eyes, a rose-leaf complexion, softly curling hair, and a smile of the most enchanting innocence. Before the end of the first evening she had managed to fascinate the whole family. She described the newest fashions with a lucidity and minuteness to which Candida had never been able to attain, gave the latest particulars of the most thrilling society scandal, appealed to Mr. St. John for information on every subject under discussion with a flattering confidence in the infallibility of his knowledge, and listened attentively to the longest of his mother's narratives about the triumphs of her youth.

"It's a pity you don't try and catch something of your friend's manner, Candida," said the old lady, after the guest had retired for the night. "She reminds me of what the girls used to be in my youth. If you would only smile and blush, and use a little more gesture while you are talking, it would add immensely to your attractions. You are not sufficiently animated for a young woman; your face and whole bearing are too impassive."

"I am very sorry," said Candida. "I only desire to be natural. I don't think the kittenish style would sit well upon me; I am too big and heavy. But Sabina is perfectly charming, as you say; men go down before her like ninepins."

That night Candida was awoke out of her first sleep by the sound of muffled sobbing in the adjoining room, which was occupied by her friend. The sobs presently increased to low moans and half-stifled cries, which seemed to be wrung from a soul in anguish. It was impossible to listen to such heartrending sounds without making some effort, at least, to administer consolation. Candida jumped out of bed, lighted a candle, tapped at the door of her friend's room, and receiving no answer, walked in.

Sabina was lying on her face, trying to stifle her sobs with the pillow, over which her beautiful hair was tossed in wild confusion.

"What's the matter now?" asked Candida, who was not wholly unused to such scenes. "You seem pretty bad."

Sabina turned on her side, and looked up with streaming eyes.

"I can't bear it," she gasped. "I'm so miserable I don't know how to live. I believe I'm going mad —stark staring mad."

Her face was white and drawn, and her eyes looked unnaturally large and dark.

"This is all about some man, I suppose," said Candida, sitting down upon the end of the bed. "Tell me as much as you like. I imagine that it does you good to talk about it."

"He doesn't care about me," went on Sabina, writhing like one in acute agony. "He never spoke a word to me last night, though he knew that we shouldn't meet again for weeks. He was with that creature all the evening, that red-haired cat, that snub-nosed demon. It is she who has come between us. I wish I had killed her before his eyes—I can't think why I didn't."

"Because you were too sensible, I should hope," said Candida. "I don't think you can be very well, Sabina. You are nervous and out of sorts. Now, if you would only work at my polymachinon for half an hour after your bath every morning, you would be a different creature at the end of a week."

Sabina broke into a shrill little laugh.

"You are too funny with your polly what's it's name," she cried. "I believe you are nothing but a great big stuffed doll. What do you know about love? Have you ever been in love, or has any one ever been in love with you?"

"No, never," replied Candida, placidly. "And when I look at you I can't say I regret it."

"Put your hand there, and you will learn something," said Sabina, pointing to the pillow with a tragic gesture.

Candida laid her hand on the pillow, and found that it was soaking wet.

"My tears," explained Sabina. "Do you propose to dry them with your polytechnicon?"

"No, but I can fetch you a dry pillow," replied her friend. "There are two in my room."

She exchanged the wet pillow for a dry one, restored the tangled bedclothes to something like order, and tucked up the love-lorn maid, who, worn out with grief and excitement, presently fell into a childlike slumber.

CHAPTER V.

The next morning Sabina awoke in the best of spirits, and sang comic songs all the time she was making her toilet. The very memory of the past night seemed to have gone from her as completely as a bad dream from one who is fully awake. Candida looked and listened in astonishment, scarcely able to believe that this was the same girl who, a few hours before, had been weeping tears of anguish.

"One can't go on being miserable about a man one is not going to see for months," explained Sabina, airily, in response to a comment from Candida upon her changed mood. "Besides, when I think about him in broad daylight he doesn't seem worth it. He is beginning to get fat, and he so often has a cold in his head. It was only his not seeming to appreciate me that made me so mad. If he had really made love to me I should have loathed him."

The visitor threw herself heart and soul into the preparations for a large garden-party which was to be given at Branksmead a day or two later. Next to

Sabina, the person who was the most excited and interested about the approaching festivity was the dowager Mrs. St. John, who apparently looked forward to a repetition of the triumphs of her youth. Her best Indian shawl was taken out of its cedarwood drawer, a new cap had been ordered from Bond Street, and every detail of her toilette had undergone the most careful and minute consideration. Meanwhile, the old lady, who had gradually been failing, mentally and physically, during the past twelve months, was stimulated to unusual liveliness and garrulity by the society of such a kindred spirit as Sabina. She chattered incessantly of the gaieties that had taken place half a century before, mixed up generations and epochs, and was sometimes so carried away by the interest of the conversation as to forget the present altogether, alluding quite naturally to the lover she had just dismissed, or the gown she meant to wear at her next ball.

Early in the afternoon of the important day she retired to her room to begin the serious business of the toilette. A few minutes later, Martin, her middle-aged attendant, came running into the drawing-room, anxious-eyed and panting for breath.

"Oh, if you please, ma'am," she gasped, "will some one come to mistress at once? She's turned so strange, I can't do nothing with her."

Candida and her mother hurried upstairs at once. They found the dowager sitting in her high-backed chair, her cap off, and her thick white hair in picturesque disorder.

"Martin," she exclaimed, her dark eyes gleaming with indignation, "how often am I to tell you that I mean to wear my new white *crêpe* bonnet with the rose-coloured feathers? Pray take away that hideous black satin erection, which looks as if it had been made for my grandmother, and get out my white silk slip and the India muslin with the pink sprig. And my hair, you stupid girl," she went on, putting up her hands to her head. "I can't think what you have done to my hair. It is all flattened down, and you seem to have smoothed my ringlets quite away. I shall never be ready in time."

Springing to her feet with unwonted agility, she peeped at herself in the glass. In an instant her expression of complacent expectancy changed, first to horrified incredulity, then to abject despair. Dropping back into her chair, she put her hands before her face, and broke into a fit of agonized weeping.

"I am old, I am old," she moaned. "Grey and wrinkled and shrunken. I had forgotten for the moment. Everything is over; there is nothing left to live for. Why do women go on living after they have lost their youth? Nobody cares about them any more. Why aren't we put out of our misery before we get to this? Shrunken and old and grey."

Her voice died away into a feeble, long-drawn wail.

Candida, her heart pierced by the sight of such helpless suffering, threw herself on her knees beside the chair, with the intention of administering consolation.

"Dear granny," she began. "You have us, and——"

She stopped short abruptly, as the old lady turned upon her with sudden fury.

"Granny!" she cried. "I know why you call me by that name; you do it to insult me, and remind me that you are young and I am old. I wish you would leave me alone. I don't want to see your insolent pink face and your great overgrown figure. Why can't I be left to die in peace?"

Candida retreated in dismay at the same moment that Mr. St. John, who had been summoned by his wife, entered the room.

"Why, what is the matter, mother?" he asked, as he bent over the unhappy old woman. "You will not be able to receive any of your admirers to-day if you don't compose yourself. Your old flame, Sir Henry Hammond, is coming on purpose to see you. He always declares that you are the most beautiful woman of your age in the kingdom."

"Sir Henry Hammond!" Mrs. St. John sat upright, and instantly composed her features, though the tears still glistened in the furrows of her cheeks. "Martin, my tea-gown and the Spanish mantilla for my head. I cannot appear in public to-day, but I will see Sir Henry in the boudoir. Some eau de Cologne and water for my eyes, and just a dust of powder. Most women would use rouge in the circumstances, but I have too much regard for my complexion. Roland, you will explain to Sir Henry that I have had an attack of nerves, but that I could not refuse to see such an old friend. Martin, don't forget to give me my fan and *vinaigrette*."

Mr. St. John beckoned to his wife and daughter to follow him from the room.

"She will soon be quite herself," he said, when they were outside. "She is tired, and has been over-excited. But if she rests for the next hour or two, it will do her no harm to see Sir Henry for a few minutes."

Candida put her hand through his arm, and leant against his shoulder. She had been strangely moved and shaken by the painful scene she had just witnessed.

"Oh, poor granny, poor granny!" she murmured. "Why is old age so intolerable and degrading to women, when it might be so beautiful and dignified?"

"Because the majority of women are brought up as if they were gifted with eternal youth, and exempted from all responsibility," he replied. "Most parents act as if they imagined that Rousseau's dictum, 'A woman should die at forty,' were carried into effect. They allow their daughters the opportunity of enjoying themselves in the sunshine of spring and summer, but give them no protection against the damp of autumn, or the frost and snow of winter. Consequently an aged woman is too often as uncomfortable an anomaly as a butterfly in December."

* * * * * *

The guests had all arrived, tennis and croquet were in full swing, and Candida, having started the games for the young people, and settled the dowagers in comfortable chairs, was standing upon the terrace, talking to the Bishop of Thorminster. The bishop, like the apostles and the four great doctors of the Church (according to ancient heraldry), was a "gentleman of blood and coat armour," who stood six foot two in his gaiters, and possessed shoulders that caused every recruiting sergeant in his diocese to break the tenth commandment. "Thor," as he was familiarly called, was the terror of clerical shirkers and absentees, but the workers adored him, and the restive spirits, who fretted under all other ecclesiastical restraint, pulled quietly and steadily when his hand was on the bridle.

The bishop had christened Candida, given her rides on his shoulder in her childish days, and confirmed her only three years before. He had been the object of her earliest hero-worship, and she still regarded him with a respectful admiration that was mainly due to his thews and sinews.

"And what church do you attend in London, my dear?" asked his lordship, at length.

Candida hesitated. The question was not altogether unexpected, and she had been debating within herself whether she could answer it without wounding the susceptibilities of a distinguished guest. The bishop had always been regarded by the ladies of the St. John household as a kind of superior pope, and therefore it was natural that she should feel a tremor at the thought of administering to him what would be, figuratively speaking, a slap in the face. But the tremor decided her. She reminded herself that she was accepting the bishop's kindness on false pretences, and that that was the conduct of a coward and a hypocrite.

"I have not attended any church for some time," she replied, with a quiver in her voice. "I think I ought to tell you, my lord, that at this moment I am not a Christian."

She held her breath like one who has just fired a train of gunpowder, and stared anxiously at the bishop's gaiters, as though expecting them to fly into the air with the shock of her communication. But, to her surprise, nothing happened, no explosion took place. The bishop merely inquired with a bland smile—

"May I be permitted to ask what you are—at this moment?"

"I don't think I am anything," replied Candida, much relieved by the calmness with which he had received her confession. "I suppose if I wished to label myself I should say that I was an agnostic, because I feel that I know nothing for certain except that we are born and that we die."

"But that ignorance is common to us all," said his lordship. "The wisest of us knows nothing for certain beyond those two well-attested facts."

Candida stared at him open-mouthed.

"We don't say 'I know' in the Creeds of our Church," he went on. "We say 'I believe,' and those words in themselves are a confession of ignorance."

"But dogmas——" stammered Candida.

"Dogmas are the drapery of faith," he replied sententiously. "Sometimes an ornament, sometimes a protection, more often an impediment. Dogmas are continually being outgrown and discarded, without the slightest injury to the living faith."

The bishop politely suppressed a yawn; he had not come to a garden-party to talk theology. His wandering eye caught sight of Sabina, the centre of a little group of admiring youths. Her tinkling laughter and their deeper "Haw haws" struck gratefully upon his ear.

"Who is the pretty young lady in the pretty hat?" he inquired. "A friend of yours? I should like to make her acquaintance."

Candida, her mind still in a whirl, introduced him to Sabina, and then walked away, feeling a little flat. If the bishop had called his fellow-guests around him, denounced her to them as an infidel, and forthwith banished her from the assembly, she would have regarded it as a perfectly just and natural proceeding. But to be smiled upon, agreed with, and then deserted for a pretty hat, was mortifying to a degree. Martyrdom might not be a pleasant experience, but at least the martyr was an important personage.

Mrs. St. John, when she had leisure to observe the course events were taking, was not altogether satisfied with the effect produced by her daughter. While Sabina was the centre of attraction, and always surrounded by obsequious males, Candida was more often to be seen among the dowagers, or talking to some middle-aged fogey. With the young men, indeed, she seemed on frank and friendly terms, but they did not pursue and surround her, follow her with their eyes, and hang upon her lips, as they did with Sabina. The mother hinted something of her disappointment to her husband.

"I was just congratulating myself upon the same thing," he replied. "It is quite refreshing to see a girl who makes no difference in her method of speaking to, or looking at, men and women. Observe Candida's composed manner, and tranquil, contented expression. As a rule, you only see that expression on the faces of women who are happily married, and the mothers of healthy children. Compare her with the other unmarried women, both young and middle-aged; note their anxious mouths, their restless eyes, their exaggerated smiles, the way they writhe and wriggle when they speak to a man. Poor things, they know that in marriage is their one chance of living, their only means of justifying their existence. If they miss that chance what have they to fall back upon but district-visiting and the mild approval of the parochial clergy? All their eggs are in one basket, and that a frail one. But with Candida the case is different. She is conscious that she has her own work in life, her own niche in the world; she can associate with men upon terms of equality because she is independent of them. Should marriage come her way, she will welcome it as one of the good gifts of life, but she will not clutch at it like a drowning wretch at a straw. I shall be glad if she has her youth calm and unharassed, free from intrigues, entanglements, and the fever of sham love-affairs. When she marries she will bring her husband a sound heart and a sound mind in a sound body."

"I shouldn't be surprised if all your wonderful theories were to end in our seeing her an old maid," said his wife, aggrievedly.

"Well, better so than that she should marry the wrong man in a hurry. But I don't think you need alarm yourself. Candida is not the sort of woman whom men leave to wither on the virgin stalk."

CHAPTER VI.

THERE was one man who had gradually come to the conclusion that it should not be his fault if Candida withered on the virgin stalk. Ted Ferrars was not a youth of impulse; he knew that it would be two or three years before he was able to support a wife, and at present his work satisfied nearly all his energies and aspirations. In the mental vision that he had formed of the future, however, the figure of his old playfellow already occupied an important place. Through the vista of the years he fancied that he could see her at his side, a brave comrade and true wife, understanding his thoughts, sympathizing with his desires, helping him in his difficulties, comforting him in his sorrows. Such was his notion of an ideal helpmate, and of this Candida seemed to him the living embodiment.

Ted had made a good start in his profession, and knew that he was already regarded as a promising young man. He was not brilliant, but he had a prodigious capacity for work, a memory upon which he could place absolute reliance, an unlimited amount of dogged determination, and, most useful of all, some influential solicitor relations. In two or three years' time he thought that, with average luck, he would be earning an income which, in addition to the allowance made him by his father, would justify him in thinking of marriage. Meanwhile, he intended to keep his hopes to himself, and refrain from pressing his suit until he had something tangible to offer. It will be seen that there was not much evidence of passion about these deliberations, nothing better than ordinary common sense and manly consideration for the woman whom he hoped to make his wife. In laying its plans, however, the one thing which youth reckons without is its own temperament.

The holidays were rapidly drawing to a close. Sabina had already left Branksmead to pay other visits, and only about ten days remained before Candida's return to town. Ted, coming up to dine at the Hall one night about this time, found the distinguished gymnast stretched upon the sofa, with her mother and aunt hovering compassionately around her. In response to his anxious inquiries, the dowager, who had temporarily recovered her clearness of mind, replied with gentle sarcasm—

"Oh, it's nothing serious; Candida has merely been fighting a brewer's drayman."

"That is rather a picturesque way of describing my little adventure," put in Candida. "You shall hear my version of the story, Ted. I saw a man brutally flogging a horse which was trying to get a heavy load of barrels up Cawston Hill. He was hitting it about the head and legs with an ash stick. You know I never can bear to see a horse ill-treated, so I politely requested him to leave off, and suggested that he and I should each put a shoulder to the wheel. Of course, he swore at me in reply, and began to beat the horse more cruelly than before. So I twisted his stick out of his hand, and said if he didn't do as I told him, I would treat him as he treated his beast. He looked as if he longed to knock me down and jump upon me, but he was smaller than I and in shocking condition, so he thought better of it, and slunk behind the cart. Then we both pushed at the wheels, and with the assistance of the horse we managed to get the load up the hill. Finally, I gave him some good advice and a shilling for his stick, and we parted on the best of terms. I'm glad he didn't show fight," she added thoughtfully; "because he looked so red and soft and shiny. If I had hit him hard anywhere, I believe he would have swelled up and died."

"I wish I had been there," said Ted, not over pleased at the anecdote. "But how did you manage to get hurt?"

"I suppose I did rather more than my share of the pushing, for I have strained my knee a little. Mother insisted on having Dr. Rose, and he says I must keep quiet for the next few days, or I shan't be fit to go back to work."

"I'm most awfully sorry," said Ted, quite incapable of expressing all the agitation that filled his breast at the sight of his deity prostrate and probably in pain.

"I wish there was anything I could do for you."

"You might give me your arm," said Candida. "I think I could hop out on to the terrace, and lie on the lounge chair. It seems such a waste to spend the whole evening indoors."

A vehement protest from her mother and aunt brought a worried look into the girl's face, which Ted, his faculties sharpened by sympathy, instantly perceived.

"I think, if Mr. St. John and I were to make a 'chair' with our crossed hands, we could carry Candida on to the terrace without jolting her," he said.

Mr. St. John agreed, and the feat was safely accomplished, in spite of Candida's fears that her weight would break their wrists. When the invalid was comfortably established in a *chaise longue*, Ted seated himself on the terrace wall by her side. His heart was beating loudly, and his breath came more quickly than usual, though not in consequence of the physical efforts he had just made. A tendril of his lady's hair had blown against his forehead in the transit, and sent the blood rushing to his brain, while the light touch of the hand that had rested upon his shoulder felt as though it were branded into his flesh.

"Isn't this unfortunate for me?" demanded Candida, who, it must be owned, made a very bad patient, having had little or no training in the art of illness. "I dare say I shall be laid on the shelf for the rest of my holiday, I who never have anything the matter with me. Doesn't it make one feel humiliated and degraded to be ailing or helpless? I suppose I'm very ungrateful, but it irritates me dreadfully to be asked incessantly how I feel, and whether I am in pain, and implored to take more care of myself. You don't mind my grumbling to you, do you, Ted? That is one of the privileges of friendship."

She smiled at him as she spoke, but he noticed that her cheeks were pale, and that there was a little crease of pain between her eyebrows. He had never before seen her wear so soft, so appealing, so feminine an air. All the chivalry in his nature rose to the surface, and his heart went out to her in yearning and tenderness. He longed to take her in his arms, and carry her safely through all the perilous paths of life. He wished that there were still dragons and giants on the earth that he might ride forth and slay them in the name of his love. He could almost have desired that she were beset by some great danger, in order that he might rescue her at the risk of his own life. For the first time his feeling for her was fired by the touch of passion, and all considerations of prudence and worldly wisdom were soon to be consumed in its flame. He could no longer keep silence, he felt irresistibly impelled to unburden his heart, even though by so doing he might put to an end to his hopes for ever.

"Always tell me everything," he cried—"all that you are thinking and feeling, all that causes you grief or pleasure. Oh, Candida—dearest!"—here a mighty sigh broke from the very depths of his heart—"I wish—I wish you would let me take care of you in future, work for you, live for you, devote my whole life to your happiness. I ask nothing better of fate, because—because I love you."

The secret was out now, and he stopped abruptly, alarmed at his own temerity. Candida, sitting bolt upright, turned upon him a pair of startled eyes.

"What are you talking about?" she cried, scarcely knowing whether to take his words seriously. "You are very obliging, but you know that I am perfectly well able to take care of myself, this little accident notwithstanding, and that I require no one to work for me. What can have put this idea into your head all of a sudden?"

"It's not sudden," he replied, a little sobered by her tone. "I have been thinking of it all the summer, but I had not intended to say anything about it for years, not until I could offer you a home. But somehow this evening, when I saw you pale and suffering, when I felt you resting on my arms, I could not keep it to myself any longer; I was obliged to speak out all that was in my heart. Don't be angry with me.

It would be such happiness only to know that you cared for me a little, that you might some day care for me more. The thought of you would make me work like a nigger, and I am sure that in two years, three at the outside, I could—we might——"

"Oh, don't talk like that," interrupted Candida, impatiently. "Of course, we ought neither of us to think of marriage for half a dozen years to come, and then we shall probably each have a different person in view. Remember, I have a profession as well as you, Ted; we are both at the beginning of a career, with one foot on the first rung of the ladder. You have made a good start, and I have excellent prospects. You know I told you that I had been studying the German and Swedish systems, and meant to try and introduce some new features at the Bloomsbury, which would probably make my name known in the profession. You ought to be able to sympathize with me, because you are very ambitious, and most enthusiastic about your own profession. How would you like to be asked to give it up almost at the outset?"

"The cases are not analogous," he replied. "I am a man, and——"

"And I am a woman," put in Candida. "That is to say, we are both human beings, both have hearts and minds, both are made of flesh and blood."

"Well," said Ted, "I suppose marriage is a profession as well as gymnastics, and the more natural for a woman. However, I won't bother you any more now. I am an obstinate sort of fellow, and I don't mean to let one rebuff frighten me. I shall bide my time, and hope for better luck a year or two hence, when habit may have quenched your rage for work."

"That's a good, sensible boy," she said, with a sigh of relief. "Six or seven years hence, if you are still in the same mind, and we are both of us free, you may ask me again; but don't make too sure of my answer."

"And you won't let this make any difference to our present friendship?"

"Oh no, you can come and see us sometimes on Sundays when we are settled in town. We shall have interesting visitors, I hope, because we don't mean to confine ourselves to one circle of acquaintance. Sabina will have her theatrical friends, and I shall invite a little dressmaker I know, who is a sort of obscure heroine, and a very original Scotch cobbler, who will like to talk socialism with you. And I hope a commissionaire who has a post in our neighbourhood will sometimes be able to come and see us. He is an old soldier, and was all through the Zulu war."

Ted looked dubious. His socialistic theories were genuine enough as regarded himself, but he was not prepared to apply them to the woman he loved.

"You two will want somebody to look after you if you are going in for such mixed society," he said. "You had better engage me to act as chucker-out."

* * * * *

Ten days later, Candida was once more upon her feet, and able to go back to her work at the appointed time. She was not allowed to enter upon an independent life without many warnings and much good advice from the various members of her family. Her grandmother recommended her always to wash her face in soft water, and presented her with a recipe for a complexion-lotion which, tradition said, had been used by the beautiful Miss Gunnings. Her aunt gave her a little book called "Continual Droppings," which contained meditations for every morning and evening in the year, and adjured her to read it diligently, that in time her spiritual stoniness might be worn away. Mrs. St. John lectured eloquently upon the dangers of wet feet and the duties of eating sufficient meat; but it was her father's parting words that impressed themselves most vividly upon Candida's mind, for the reason that they caused her some little surprise and distress.

"You are very young to be starting upon an independent career, my child," he began. "Still, the world presents fewer perils and temptations to a young woman than to a young man, if only because she is gifted with a colder temperament, and has acquired an abnormal power of self-restraint, the result of centuries of repression of all natural ideas, feelings, and instincts on the part of her sex. I have every faith in your good sense and right judgment, but I should like to give you a word of warning against your friend."

"Against Sabina!" said Candida, opening her eyes. "Why, I thought you liked her so much."

"She is a most lovely and delightful young lady," he replied. "And her mere proximity is enough to make an old man feel young again. But she is essentially a creature of emotion. She will always be swayed, guided, inspired by impulse; neither principles nor moral codes exist for her. She combines all the acquired weakness of a woman with much of the natural fire of a man. It is women such as she who change the fate of nations, and set kingdoms in a blaze. Wise men run mad for them, and princes lay crowns and sceptres at their feet."

"But how does all that affect me?" asked his daughter. "I know that Sabina is fascinating, and I admit that she may sometimes be foolish, but neither her fascination nor her folly can harm me."

"I see," said Mr. St. John, "that when we try to graft foreign qualities upon a character, we run the risk of losing indigenous ones. Your training has freed you from many of the weaknesses that are supposed to be natural to the feminine temperament, but at the same time you appear to be lacking in certain of the gifts that have always stood woman in good stead. You have lost the intuitive knowledge of your own sex, a loss for which only long and varied experience can ever compensate you. You are attracted, and will probably be deceived by exactly the same kind of girl who would attract and deceive a man. You believe in your friend upon the same grounds that a man believes in his sweetheart, namely, because she is pretty and amiable. No doubt Miss Romney is attached to you, and she will probably be true to you as long as her emotions are not brought into play. If ever a man comes between you, beware of your pretty Sabina."

"I am quite willing to take the risk," laughed Candida. "Sabina is welcome to all the lovers. I have other things to think about."

CHAPTER VII.

It was on a misty October afternoon that the two friends settled down into their new home, three little rooms in Blake Street, one of the dingiest thoroughfares in Bloomsbury.

"I do like living in lodgings," said Sabina, as she flitted about, filling vases and jugs with flowers that had been brought from Branksmead. "It always reminds me of holidays at the seaside. As long as we are indoors there is nothing to show that we are not at Brighton. And the best of having only one sitting-room," she added, "is that one can always keep a plum-cake in the cupboard."

"I think the room will look rather pretty when the pictures are up," said Candida. "Ted is coming to-morrow to help us to hang them."

She spoke without a trace of self-consciousness; indeed, she felt none, for Ted had returned to his former friendly attitude, and she had succeeded in putting his premature declaration out of her mind.

"To think that I really begin work on my own account on Monday!" she said with a radiant face, as they sat at tea. "Only two days more, and I shall actually be 'spinning my own free hours,' a burden upon no man."

"You'll sing a different tune after twelve months of it," said Sabina. "I was thanking the fates that the theatre doesn't open for another fortnight. I feel sometimes like the maid-of-all-work in the epitaph; I long to 'do nothing for ever and ever.'"

"That is because you have no real taste for your profession," said Candida. "You were forced into it through circumstances. But I wonder, feeling as you do, that you don't marry. I am sure you have plenty of opportunity."

"Perhaps I would if I could find a man to love me," answered Sabina, with unusual earnestness. "Oh, I know I've plenty of lovers, but not one of them cares for me—my own self—the real Sabina; they are only in love with my looks. You don't know how sick I get of being told I'm pretty. There comes a time in my acquaintance with nearly every man when he thinks proper to inform me of that fact, as if it were quite a new discovery. He seems to imagine that I shall be so overwhelmed with gratitude at the announcement, that I shall instantly lose my heart to him in return. I suppose they all take it for granted that I have a pretty little soul to match my pretty little body. There is not one who wouldn't turn from me if I had the small-pox, or had been guilty of theft or murder."

"Well, you could hardly expect a man to love a criminal," said Candida.

"Why not? A woman can. If I loved a man I shouldn't care if he had robbed a church, or killed his own brother. But the vilest man in creation always expects to have an immaculate woman for his wife."

The time that followed was a period of hard work and rigid economy for our heroine; yet, in later days, as her father had prophesied, she looked back upon those strenuous months as among the happiest of her life. She was young, strong, unharassed by heart-burnings of whatsoever kind, enjoyed her work, and was proud of her position as a unit in the universal army of labour. Lack of time and lack of money, rather than lack of inclination, prevented her from going into society, apart from occasional tea or supper-parties at the houses of hard-working women like herself. On Sunday afternoons the little sitting-room in Graham Street was chiefly filled with Sabina's friends, though Ted Ferrars was a pretty constant visitor. Candida's plan of mixing the classes and the masses had proved a decided failure, not on account of the haughtiness of the classes, but by reason of the bashfulness of the masses. On the only occasion when the two sections of society fairly met, the representatives of the classes had so lionized, patronized, pestered and petted the representatives of the masses, that the latter, bewildered and ashamed, had fled on the earliest opportunity, and obstinately refused to repeat the experiment. Candida, however, was a welcome guest in the houses of several of her poorer neighbours, being, as one of them informed her, "a nice, homely sort of young woman, who never poked her nose into things as didn't concern her, nor gave her opinion afore it was asked." Help she could only give to her less prosperous sisters in kind, teaching musical drill on one evening in the week at an institute for working girls.

During those first few months of independence, although her number of private pupils gradually increased, Candida found it a pretty hard task to make both ends meet. Nearly the whole of her earnings were swallowed up in the expenses of board and lodging, omnibus fares, and other small necessaries, leaving an almost imperceptible margin for dress or pocket-money. Boots had to be patched, gloves worn shiny, and all *menus plaisirs* rigorously foregone. Almost her only recreation consisted of an occasional visit to concerts or theatres with orders which were as plentiful as blackberries in Sabina's circle of acquaintance.

In her profession Candida was modestly conscious of being a success. Her pupils bestowed upon her a good measure of heroine-worship, that frankest and most unalloyed of youthful emotions. They laughed it is true, at the severe felt hat and shabby serge coat and skirt which constituted her invariable outdoor attire; but they raved about her figure and her hair, and agreed that whatever she wore she looked "perfectly splendid." The secret of her success was probably due to the enthusiasm that she felt for her work, as well as to her earnest belief in its usefulness as a factor in the progress of her own sex, and through it of the whole race. Nothing gave her more gratification than to see the girls who came to the gymnasium in the giggling, hysterical, anæmic stage, transformed under her eyes into strong, healthy women, firm of muscle, steady of nerve, and supple of form.

The two friends lived amicably together, the more so, perhaps, for seeing very little of each other, even their meals being for the most part at different hours. Only one dispute disturbed their peace in the course of the winter, and in that Candida admitted that she was to blame. Coming home late one bitter night from the Working Girls' Institute, she perceived what looked like a heap of clothes huddled up on the doorstep. Bending down, she found that the heap was a woman, whose face was turned away from the lamplight.

"I'm afraid you are ill," said Candida, gently. "Can I do anything for you?"

The woman turned round sharply, and instantly assumed a defensive attitude.

"I'm not doing any harm," she said hoarsely. "I only sat down a minute to get my breath. I went kind of dizzy, but I ain't drunk; you'd smell my breath if I was. You've no call to tell me to move on."

A violent fit of coughing interrupted her speech, and she rocked herself to and fro, gasping for breath, while the handkerchief which she held to her lips was spotted with blood.

"You poor thing!" said Candida, shocked at the woman's evident expectation of rough usage. "I'm only anxious to help you. You will kill yourself if you sit out here in the cold with that dreadful cough. If you will come in with me you can rest and warm yourself by the fire, and afterwards you will feel better able to walk home."

"Are you one of them good lydies what gets hold of people and tries to keep them in?" asked the woman.

"No, I am not at all good, and I am only a working girl. If you will make use of my room till you feel better, you will be perfectly free to go your way."

"Do you know what sort of a woman I am?" asked the other, suspiciously.

"Yes," answered Candida, promptly. "I know that you are a sick woman, and that if you sit out here much longer you are likely to be a dead woman. Will you let me help you upstairs, and give you some supper?"

She raised the panting creature in her strong arms, half carried her up the stairs, and established her on the sofa near the fire. Then she warmed up some soup, and brought a cup to her visitor, who drank it eagerly.

"That's real good stuff," she said with a sigh. "I've had nothing all day but a crust of bread and a pennyworth of 'thick.'"

Candida brought her a plate of cold beef next, but the woman tried in vain to choke down a mouthful of meat.

"It's no good," she said; "my teeth are bad, and my stomach's weak. I ain't used to solid food, but I could do with another cup of that soup."

Candida warmed up the remainder of the soup, and then brought out a bottle of port wine which had been bought on account of a sore throat of Sabina's. The warmth of the room, the food, and a glass of wine put the visitor into a state of drowsiness from which she had just passed into an uneasy slumber when Sabina returned from the theatre very cold and a little cross.

"Who on earth have you got there?" she asked, gazing at the figure with such manifestly disapproving eyes that Candida began to feel suddenly uncomfortable.

"It's a poor sick woman whom I found on the doorstep," she explained. "And I brought her in for a little food and warmth."

"Good heavens!" cried Sabina, "have you taken leave of your senses? She was probably drunk. And how do you know she is respectable?"

"She is quite sober," answered Candida. "I can't answer for her respectability, but she certainly has bronchitis."

"You've finished the soup between you, I see, and I do believe you've been giving her some of my port wine. She may be sober, but no respectable woman would be sitting on doorsteps at this time of night."

"*Bother* respectability!" cried Candida, who had a deep-mouthed way of pronouncing the harmless expletive that made it almost as effective as an oath. " Have you got no feelings of humanity? Can't you realize that she is a woman like ourselves, made of the same flesh and blood, with the same capacity for suffering, the same need of kindness and sympathy? Do you grudge her the little we can give her, just because she is ill and in distress? You don't grudge your hospitality to people who fare sumptuously every day."

"Oh well, you needn't excite yourself," said Sabina, sitting down to her supper. "But perhaps you'll kindly explain what you mean to do with her now that you have fed and warmed her. I'm afraid twopence and promises wouldn't go far with any inn-keeper in these days."

"She said she wanted to go home," answered Candida, doubtfully. "But it has begun to snow again, and the wind is worse than ever. It would be like committing a murder to turn her out now.

Perhaps if we kept her till to-morrow morning we could persuade her to go into a refuge or infirmary."

At these words the woman on the sofa opened her eyes, and moved uneasily

"For Gawd's sake, lady, don't put me into no refuges!" she said. "I've been there; I know all about 'em. They're always at you about your sins, and the love of Jesus, and they makes you feel bad inside all for nothing. I shan't last much longer," she added drowsily; "but I mean to die in the open."

"You shall do just as you please," said Candida. "But I hope you will remain here to-night, and to-morrow we will see if we can do anything to help you, to make you more comfortable."

She fetched a warm rug from her bedroom, and wrapped it round the shrunken figure of the woman, who was soon asleep again.

"I suppose you would like to support her for the remainder of her existence," said Sabina, sarcastically.

Candida looked at her with a wistful glance.

"I believe we could do it if we lived on porridge," she said. "The poor creature was right in saying that she would not last long. There is death in her face."

"Well, I haven't the slightest intention of living on porridge, or of sharing a lodging with a woman picked out of the gutter," said Sabina. "As it is, the landlady will probably give us notice to-morrow.

I'm going to bed. Do you mean to leave your guest alone here, in order that she may pocket what she pleases in the morning?"

"No, I shall put on my dressing-gown, and sleep in an armchair. We can't disturb the poor creature now. She shall be left in peace for a few hours, at least."

Candida, tired with a hard day's work, slept soundly on her improvised bed, and did not awake until half-past seven, her usual hour of rising. As the events of the past night slowly returned to her mind, she glanced anxiously round the room; but it was empty. The guest must have stolen away in the early winter dawn, scared by the prospect of being delivered over to the tender mercies of the good. A deliberate scrutiny of the room revealed the fact that she had taken nothing with her. The little ornaments on the mantel-piece were undisturbed; the tale of the spoons and forks was complete.

With a heavy heart Candida went off to her morning's work. On her return to the midday dinner, she was informed by Sabina that the outraged landlady, who had somehow got wind of her lodger's strange proceedings, had expressed her intention of giving them notice to quit the next time that they brought in " creatures " out of the street.

"She means it, too," concluded Sabina. "She has cherished a grudge against you, Candida, ever since you took the last slavey but one to the

Ophthalmic Hospital, and brought her home in spectacles. What a row there was when the old lady refused to let her wear them! I never realized till then what a fearful temper you had."

"Any display of temper was justified by her diabolical behaviour," cried Candida, flushing with indignation at the remembrance. "I wasn't going to allow the wretched child to lose her sight for a mere whim. The barbarous old hag, to say that she couldn't have a servant of hers doing her work in spectacles!"

"So you gave the old hag a piece of your mind, and she gave the slavey a month's warning. And the end of the matter was that you had to pawn your watch in order to support the girl till she got another place."

"Yes, that was rather inconvenient," admitted Candida. "But in the end I found her a situation with some human beings, who are rather proud of having a spectacled servant; they think it makes her look like a lady-help. I don't regret my action in that case at all, but I am willing to admit that I may sometimes be too impulsive and unpractical. I had no right to bring that woman last night into a room which I share with another person, particularly if that other person were likely to object. I ought to have given her some food at a restaurant, and sent her home in a cab. But it cut me to the heart to see her evident expectation of harshness and cruelty, when I, another woman, spoke to her. She seemed to think that because she was ill and in misery it was natural that I should treat her with cold-blooded brutality. Oh!" she went on, with sudden passion, "I feel sometimes as if all the wretchedness in London were resting on my shoulders, and I could not lift a finger to lighten the burden. I daren't think, I daren't listen, I daren't look to the right hand or to the left when I walk through the streets. The sound of

> 'Women sobbing out of sight
> Because men made the laws'

seems to be always in my ears."

"I don't see why you should worry yourself about it," said Sabina. "You have no time, or money, or influence. You can't do anything."

"No, not now," admitted Candida, mournfully. "I can do nothing but feel for them. But if I live, I'll do something for them some day, when I am older and wiser, and have conquered in the struggle for life. It may be twenty years before I'm ready, but I shall be gaining experience, preparing myself all the time. I can be patient, but if I can help it, I won't go out of the world without having broken a lance on behalf of my sisters, who are made the victims and scapegoats of society."

"I don't recommend you to wait too long," observed Sabina, with her little cynical smile—"at least, if you want men to help you. If you wait till you have lost your looks, you may talk till you are black in the face, and however eloquent your pleading, however admirable your cause, no man will heed you."

CHAPTER VIII.

IN the course of the spring, Candida received disquieting accounts of her grandmother's health from time to time. The old lady was evidently failing rapidly, both in mind and body, so that it was with but little surprise that the girl received a telegram one morning, early in May, summoning her to Branksmead, to take a last leave of her grandmother.

A few hours later she drove up to the door of her own home, where her father was looking out for her.

"Lester will have told you that you are just in time," he said. "But the doctors think that she can scarcely live through the night."

"Let me go to her at once," said Candida, in awed tones, for this was the first time that Death had laid his hand upon one who was near to her, and warm though the life-blood was in her veins, it made her realize his power.

She slipped her hand through her father's arm, and together they went upstairs to the sick-room. As the door opened Candida heard the faint sound of a murmuring voice. Her grandmother, wearing a nightgown that seemed composed entirely of embroidery and tucks, and a cap trimmed with fine old lace, was talking softly to herself, as she lay among her pillows, and picked at the counterpane with transparent fingers. Her finely cut aquiline nose looked pinched, and there were faint grey shadows round her mouth and eyes; otherwise Candida thought her but little altered. Her daughter was kneeling beside the bed, her face hidden in her hands.

"Your mother has gone to lie down," whispered Mr. St. John. "She was up all last night."

"It must be nearly time to start," the dying woman was saying to herself. "We must get there early, or my best partners will have their cards filled up. I shall look like a *débutante* to-night in this white gown, but they say that white suits me better than any colour. I promised Sir James the first waltz. Will he speak to-night, I wonder? A little encouragement—after supper—and I ought to be able to bring him to the point."

She stopped to give a little laugh of triumph.

Miss Agnes raised an agonized face to her brother.

"Can nothing be done to bring her to a sense of her frightful peril?" she asked. "This worldly talk is too horrible when we know that in a few hours she will be plunged into eternity. I have sent for Mr. Oriel; I hoped he would have been here before now."

"Poor soul, she seems quite happy and peaceful," said Mr. St. John. "It seems a pity to disturb her."

"I hope I'm in looks to-night," went on the sick woman. "The Leveson girl is to be there, and they say she is quite a belle, with a waist of eighteen inches. But Sir James declares——"

"Mr. Oriel is here," answered a voice at the door.

"Thank God!" cried Miss Agnes, devoutly. "Beg him to come in at once, Martin."

The young curate entered, a big Prayer-book under his arm, and a scared expression on his face.

"Oh, Mr. Oriel," said the afflicted daughter, "do speak to her; do try and lead her mind to holy thoughts."

Thus adjured, the unhappy curate cautiously approached the bed. The sight of a masculine figure attracted the invalid's attention.

"I don't think I've met you before," she remarked, staring up at him. "Or were you introduced to me at the Hunt ball? I'm afraid I can't give you a dance to-night; my programme is quite full. Besides," she added in a would-be aside, "I never dance with parsons."

"My dear sister," began the young man, in trembling tones, "let me exhort you to turn your thoughts in this awful hour to things that may be of comfort and healing to your soul. Remember that there is time, even at the eleventh hour, for all who truly——"

"What is he mumbling about now?" demanded the old lady, sharply. "If it's eleven o'clock it's high time the carriage came round. The first waltz will be over before we get there, and I promised Sir James I would be punctual."

"You see she is in no state to benefit by your ministrations," whispered Mr. St. John. "But if you like to kneel down somewhere out of sight, and read some prayers in a low tone, it will be a comfort to my sister, and can do the patient no harm."

The curate, with evident relief, retired behind the cheval-glass, and began to read extracts from the service for the Visitation of the Sick, which mingled strangely with the wanderings of the person for whose benefit they were intended.

"I hope my hair is quite firm," she muttered, trying to raise one hand to her head. "That new polka mazurka is enough to shake out all one's hairpins. I came home from the last assembly dance with my wreath hanging over one ear; Colonel Gaythorpe said I looked like a Bacchante."

"Sanctify, we pray thee, this thy fatherly correction to her," monotoned the curate, "that the sense of her weakness may add strength to her faith, and seriousness to her repentance."

"I feel rather breathless," went on the voice from the bed. "I'm afraid I made Bellman lace me too tight. But I told her she must draw me in to seventeen inches, because the Leveson girl is eighteen. I hope the lace won't break; it might injure my prospects for life."

"Consider her contrition," came from behind the cheval-glass. "Accept her tears, assuage her pain, as shall seem most expedient to thee."

The montonous reading seemed to soothe the patient, who presently fell into a drowsy state, which lasted for several hours. Candida, who had been sent to lie down at ten o'clock, was roused soon after midnight by her mother.

"She is awake now," said Mrs. St. John; "and I think the end must be very near."

When they reached the sick-room, they found the dying woman in a most enviable frame of mind. Her beautiful dark eyes were shining like stars, and there was a radiant smile upon her lips.

"He has come to the point at last," she was saying, "and everything is settled. He has twenty thousand a year, a place in Berkshire, and a house in Grosvenor Square. The settlements are all that could be wished, the family diamonds are to be reset, and all the other girls are mad with envy."

She closed her eyes with a long-drawn sigh of happiness, sank back upon her pillows, and before sunrise had gently breathed her life away.

This death-bed scene, the first that she had ever witnessed, made a deep impression on Candida's mind. She had fancied that death must always of necessity be solemn, tragic, mysterious, and that the aged, at least, were prepared to meet the great change with dignity and calm acquiescence, having renounced all hold upon the world and the infinite littleness of finite life. But now she discovered that dying could be conducted in almost as frivolous a fashion as living. She had felt sickened and ashamed during the great last scene that should have inspired nothing but awe, while the solemn mummeries of the funeral had almost moved her to an outbreak of hysterical laughter. The obtrusive quiet of the undertaker's men, the difficulties of all the mourners with the buttons of their new kid gloves, the abnormally developed manes and tails of the horses, the magnificent flowers which were solemnly deposited in the grave, as though the dead woman were expected to carry a bouquet when she made her *début* into the next world,—all these things made the girl feel as if death were but an undignified continuation of the farcical comedy of life.

One day, shortly after the funeral, her father found her sitting alone upon her favourite garden-seat, an expression of puzzled despondency upon her face.

"You are troubled and depressed," he said, seating himself beside her. "It is only to be expected; you have just had your first sight of death."

"It is not death that troubles me," she answered. "Death seems natural and comprehensible enough.

It is life that I find so perplexing. I was wondering whether granny was still alive somewhere, and if so, how much she was changed. I cannot imagine her being happy in paradise without a looking-glass, unless she were transformed into somebody else. And if she is to be somebody else to all eternity, why should she have been herself during these few years upon earth?"

"You want to know too much," said her father. "It is the fashion of the age to ask unanswerable questions, and then to be miserable because there is no reply. Egoism and curiosity are the distinguishing characteristics of the period. Our vocabulary will soon be reduced to two words, 'I,' and 'Why.'"

"But there must be answers to all these questions, if we could only find them out," returned Candida. "Why should not some, at least, be solved in our lifetime?"

"Why not? Life seems long at twenty," said the squire, smiling. "Let me suggest a possible answer to one of your riddles now. You ask why your grandmother should have been herself in this life, when it is probable that if she still exists, she will be somebody quite different to all eternity? I reply that she never was herself in this life, except perhaps during her earliest childhood. She, like most other women, was the purely artificial product of a lopsided civilization which has been built up by one sex, and of an age in which one sex has reigned supreme. It may be that in another existence these victims of society may have a chance of continuing the growth that was checked and stunted in this life. Here they never get beyond mental childhood, there they may be allowed to attain their full stature."

"That is a consoling theory, certainly," said Candida. "But it would be better practice to grant them freedom to grow as high as they can in the only life they are quite sure of."

The long summer holidays passed uneventfully away. The return to town was followed by an increase of work and an increase of income. A rise in salary, and a few more private pupils obviated the necessity for such rigid economy as Candida had been compelled to practise during the preceding winter. The preparations for a grand public performance and prize-giving which was to be held at the Gymnasium early in the new year, kept her busily employed New exercises were to be introduced, and extra classes were held to enable the pupils to practise for the important event. Candida had no time for doubts or questionings, and her spiritual perplexities quickly disappeared before the realities of work-a-day life.

CHAPTER IX.

ON a foggy day early in January, two young men were lunching together at a restaurant in Holborn. Their tongues went even faster than their knives and forks, for they were talking that financial "shop" which is so enthralling to the initiated, and by reason of its technical jargon so fearsomely mysterious to the outsider.

"Got anything particular to do this afternoon, Sylvester?" asked the elder, as he beckoned up the waiter.

"No," replied the other, rather gloomily. "There is no object in going back to the old shop this afternoon. Fred is there, but there's absolutely nothing doing. No one dares touch anything. I never saw the market in such a state."

"Then there's bound to be a reaction soon," said his friend, more cheerfully. "The slump can't last much longer, and when the luck turns we'll all make our fortunes. You had better come with me this afternoon. I'm going to inspect one of the places where they manufacture new women, and I can take you in too, if you like."

"Doesn't sound much in my line, nor in yours either, Travers. Is it a Women's Suffrage Meeting, or what?"

"No, it's a field-day at a girls' gymnasium. A young cousin of mine is a pupil there, and she says one of the instructors is uncommonly good-looking, with the best figure in London. Of course, you can't trust a girl's judgment in such matters; but as I've nothing particular to do, I thought I'd look in for half an hour. There's to be skirt-dancing as well as gymnastics, and altogether I imagine it will be something like a highly respectable music-hall with the songs left out."

"H'm!" said Sylvester, dubiously. "That doesn't sound wildly exciting. Still, I don't mind going with you as long as it's only for half an hour. I suppose they won't allow us to smoke."

Candida, though she had no time to think about it, happened to be looking her best that afternoon. Her cheeks were pink, her eyes sparkling, her fair hair slightly ruffled, and her whole face lit up with animation and excitement. Her costume, a well-cut tunic and knickerbockers of smoke-blue, with a silken sash loosely knotted round the waist, became her far better than ordinary feminine attire. She had lately been unexpectedly promoted, owing to the marriage of one of the other instructors, and was now second in command. Her "chief" being occupied in receiving guests and superintending the general arrangements, most of the practical work fell upon Candida. It was she who had to put the squadrons through the musical drill, and display to best advantage the various feats upon the vaulting-horse, parallel bars, swings, and ladders, encouraging the timid, covering the mistakes of the clumsy, and stimulating the "show pupils" to the highest pitch of excellence.

While the skirt-dancing was going on she had leisure to look about her, and recognize her friends among the audience. Her glance, wandering carelessly over the rows of spectators, was arrested by the dark eyes and pale handsome face of a young man whom she had previously remarked as being one of the most eager in interest and vehement in applause. He must be a friend of the Travers's, she decided, for she had noticed that Mabel Travers had smiled and nodded at him. He looked ill and worn, yet he was certainly very picturesque. How he stared! She met his eyes every time she glanced in his direction until the skirt-dancing came to an end, and she was called away to make arrangements for the high jump.

Meanwhile, Adrian Sylvester had been so carried away by his enthusiastic admiration for the "girl in blue" that his friend Travers had been obliged to try and check his raptures by pointing out that he was making an ass of himself, and attracting more attention than any of the performers. But Adrian, having

Irish blood in his veins, was but little afflicted with *mauvaise honte.* He would restrain himself for a minute or two, and then break out again with—

"But she's superb, she's matchless, she's unique! Can't you see it, old fellow? Haven't you got any eyes in your head? Those lines, those curves, those attitudes! It's Freija herself come back to earth."

"Fry—how much?" asked Travers. "A fine, strapping young woman, no doubt; but have you noticed that little witch in the front row, the one with fluffy hair and mauve in her hat?"

"That—pooh, a doll, a fashion-plate," returned his friend, contemptuously. "But this other; look how she stands and moves! Now she's carrying that jumping apparatus across the room. Did you ever see such a poise, such poetry of motion? Can't you appreciate the turn of her head, and that pillar of a throat, and the way her hair crests up from the parting? Here, where's my pencil? I must try and get that effect."

For a few minutes he sketched rapidly, with bold firm strokes, while his friend looked admiringly over his shoulder.

"Yes, that's not bad," said Travers, at length. "You've got the general effect right enough. I always said you ought to have gone in for art, only I suppose you'd never have had the patience to grind at that any more than at anything else."

After the performance there was tea in the class-room for the guests and the teachers. Adrian lost no time in getting hold of Travers's aunt, and making her introduce him to Miss St. John, who was helping to pour out the tea.

"I have been longing to tell you how much I have enjoyed this afternoon," he said eagerly. "The whole thing has been quite a revelation to me. These girls are just as strong and active as boys, and they seem to take quite as much pleasure in violent exercise. I always thought that they preferred dressing dolls and reading story-books to any active amusements."

"That is the most firmly rooted of all fallacies," said Candida, smiling at the *naiveté* of his manner. "From their earliest childhood girls are told that it is tomboyish to run and jump and climb, and taught that all properly behaved young ladies ought to sit still and sew their seam or read their book. Of course, the poor little twigs grow the way they are bent; but once give them a chance of sprouting in a natural direction, and they are only too ready to take advantage of it. Did I see you making sketches just now?" she added, thinking that he could not really be interested in the subject of feminine education. "Were you doing them for a paper?"

"No, only for my own amusement. I am the merest amateur."

He took out his note-book, and opened it at the page which contained the most successful study of herself.

"Did I really look like that?" she asked, in pleased surprise. "I had no idea that I could ever look so—so nice. But, apart from all question of resemblance, it seems to me a very clever sketch. May I look at some of the others?"

He turned over the leaves for her, and together they laughed at one or two caricatures of stout, clumsy girls who had twisted themselves into extraordinary contortions in the conscientious effort to perform some difficult feat. The sketches led Adrian to ask for information about some of the exercises with clubs and bar-bells that had particularly taken his fancy; but before his companion could enlighten him very far she was called away to attend to other visitors. Just before his departure, however, the young man contrived to get another word with her.

"I was so awfully interested in what you were telling me just now," he said. "I should have liked to hear a lot more, because I want to try some of those things myself. I don't get half enough exercise to keep me in health."

He paused, and looked at her with soft wistful eyes. Even had she been less attracted by him than she was, Candida could hardly have refused the invitation he was so evidently angling for.

"If you will come and see us some Sunday at tea-time, I will tell you all I can," she answered cordially. "Our address is 197, Blake Street."

On the Sunday week following, Candida was

unwillingly entertaining a visitor of whom she had seen a good deal more than she desired during the past few months. This was a certain Professor Harding, an Oxford don, and a personage of some celebrity in his own sphere. The professor was rather an unfinished-looking specimen of humanity, with a narrow chest and short legs, weak sight and a scanty growth of hair; but, like many of his kind, he was blessed with a magnifying eye where his own personality was concerned. He always walked on tip-toe, bowed his head on entering a door of average height, and evidently saw himself in imagination as a man of imposing presence, and more than ordinary strength. He cherished a theoretical enthusiasm for physical culture, for Nature, and for poetry of the robust school, frankly declaring himself a pagan in temperament, and an enemy of civilization. He had professed an immense admiration for Candida from the first moment of their acquaintance. In appearance she was his feminine ideal, he openly averred; he had never before seen any woman so purely, so completely Greek. He was sure that in a former incarnation she must have raced with Atalanta, or played at ball with Nausicaa.

The languid raptures of this puny admirer inspired his idol with nothing but irritation and distaste. She did her best to avert a threatened declaration by laughing at his Neo-Hellenism, disagreeing with his artistic theories, refusing to share his contempt for all good work that lay outside his own narrow canons of taste, and even declaring herself unable to appreciate Walt Whitman. This last heresy had almost sent the professor back to Oxford cured of his infatuation; but the thought that his eloquence might enable him to make a convert of this splendid young Philistine brought him once again to Blake Street with an expression of determination in his watery eyes that made his hostess's heart quail within her, for Sabina had fled, and she shrank from making herself positively unpleasant in her own house. However, geniality, she felt, would be fatal, so she sat and listened with but the faintest pretence of interest while her admirer endeavoured to entertain her with highly coloured word-sketches of the Alpine scenery amid which he had spent his summer vacation.

"I'm afraid you hardly sympathize with my feeling for Nature," he said at length, perceiving that his efforts scarcely met with the appreciation that he considered their due. "I hope you are not a disciple of Peter Bell."

"I believe I am," replied Candida, eagerly seizing another opportunity of proving her heterodoxy. "At least, a primrose by the river's brim, or anywhere else, a yellow primrose is to me, and nothing more. I don't see why it should be any more; it certainly would not have any greater attractions for me if I could see a moral lesson in it. It strikes me that nowadays Nature suffers more from her admirers than from those who are simply indifferent to her. I am thinking of the persons who find lectures in stones, magazine articles in the running brooks, and self-advertisement in everything. They patronize the Alps, write puff-paragraphs about the first daffodil, and are always ready to do the honours of a fine sunset."

"But the interpreters of Nature," began the little man. "Surely we owe something——"

"I don't see that Nature needs any interpreters," put in Candida. "If we are blind to her beauties, no interpreter can give us eyes; but it is a mistake to suppose that those who look and admire in silence are less appreciative than the self-constituted word-painters, who vulgarize the most exquisite landscapes by trying to lithograph them in crudely-coloured language. I am often reminded, when I read modern descriptive writing, of Lowell's remark that 'if everybody must needs blab of the favours that have been done him by roadside and river-brink and woodland walk, as if to kiss and tell were no longer treachery, it will be a positive refreshment to meet a man who is as superbly indifferent to Nature as she is to him.'"

"How brutally I'm behaving," she added to herself, remorsefully. "Still, it's the truest kindness in his case, for a refusal would be a crushing blow to his vanity."

Fortunately, before her admirer could think of a suitable reply to this attack upon Nature's self-complacent showmen, the door opened, and Mr. Sylvester was announced. The cordiality with which the new-comer was received put the finishing touch to the professor's displeasure. After sitting for a few moments in sulky silence, he took his departure, carefully explaining that as he was returning to Oxford on the following day, it would probably be a long time before he had the pleasure of meeting Miss St. John again.

When Adrian found himself alone with his hostess, he drew his chair nearer to hers, and said in confidential tones—

"I've bought a pair of dumb-bells."

"I'm delighted to hear it," she answered, amused at his evident expectation of her interest and sympathy. "If you practise with them regularly I'm sure you'll feel the better for it."

"It's precious dull work," he observed ruefully. "They want musical accompaniments, such as you have at your gymnasium, to make them go down. I'm awfully fond of music; perhaps you'll let me try your piano some day."

"What, you're a musician as well as an artist?" said Candida. "How many more accomplishments do you possess?"

"Oh, I only just strum a little, chiefly by ear," he answered modestly. "And as for drawing, I—I—er——"

He paused, and put his hand to his head. Candida noticed that he had turned deadly white.

"You are not feeling well," she cried anxiously. "Your head is bad."

"Oh, it's nothing—nothing to speak of," he answered faintly. "Only the room is rather warm, and coming in out of the cold I—I——"

His voice failed again, and, to his hostess's dismay, he gradually slipped from his chair, and subsided on to the floor. Candida ran to the window, and threw it open, then placed a cushion under the head of the unconscious youth, and dashed some water from a flower-vase in his face. As she did so, she was again struck by the clear-cut beauty of his features, in spite of their ashen pallor.

In a few moments he began to revive. The dark eyes opened, and fixed themselves upon her face.

"Violet," he murmured softly, "you have come back to me."

Candida made no reply, but contented herself with chafing his cold hands in her warm ones. As the faintness gradually passed away, he raised his head, and stared round him in dazed perplexity.

"I'm damned if I know where I am," he said in more natural tones. "Have I been drinking again?"

"No, no," cried Candida, quickly. "You are with me—Miss St. John. The room was too warm, and it made you feel a little faint."

A hot flush of shame stole over his face.

"Good heavens, what must you think of me!" he

cried. "How could I make such a fool of myself, and give you all this trouble?"

"You mustn't talk like that," she said kindly. "Come, let me help you on to the sofa. You must lie still till you feel quite recovered, and then I will send for a cab."

"How good you are to me!" he said gratefully, as he lay back upon the cushions of the sofa. "My mother would like to thank you if she knew."

There was a change in his voice as he spoke of his mother that went to Candida's heart.

"You are her only son?" she asked.

He nodded.

"And she is a widow," he answered softly.

"You ought to take care of yourself for her sake. You don't look very strong."

"Oh, I'm pretty tough," he said carelessly. "I don't want you to think me a chronic invalid. Shall I tell you what really made me feel so queer to-day?" he added impulsively, a twinkle dawning in his eyes.

"Yes, if you don't mind my knowing."

"You promise not to be shocked?"

"Yes, if it's not very shocking."

"Well, then, I didn't get to bed till past four this morning, and I've had nothing all day but some soda-water and a biscuit."

"Oh," cried Candida, "how can you destroy your health in that fashion? Do I know you well enough to say that you are very wrong and very foolish?"

"You may call me whatever names you please," he answered cheerfully. "I know I'm playing the deuce with my health, but I can't help it; I'm driven to it. The other fellows in my set do just the same, and I can't keep out of it; I wasn't cut out for a hermit. I'm sure there are times when I feel sick enough of it all, when the whole thing bores me to death—whisky, and cards, and music-halls, and all the rest of it. Yet I can't mope at home every evening; I'm such a sociable beast. And, after all, one can only enjoy one's self while one's young."

"But it seems a pity to use up youth and strength as you are doing without getting any real enjoyment in return," said Candida, secretly flattered at the confidence that had been reposed in her. "Don't you know any pleasant houses where you can drop in in the evening when you've nothing particular to do, without waiting to be asked?"

"No, I haven't a general invitation to any house I should care to go to in that sort of way; I wish I had. But, you see, I'm not an eligible, and so mothers don't encourage me. As a rule, I spend my evenings between the club and the music-halls. But that sort of thing gets frightfully monotonous after a time."

"You ought to go on the river or play golf when you can get the chance," said Candida, thoughtfully, for she was becoming interested in this good-looking young penitent; "then you wouldn't feel tempted to sit up playing cards till four in the morning. And if you were to get some Indian clubs you would find them more interesting than dumb-bells, especially if you had any one to play accompaniments for you."

Her words sounded cold and unsympathetic in her own ears. This youth was a complete stranger to her; yet he had allowed her a glimpse into the trials and temptations of his life. Stranger or not, he was a human soul in a fair way to ruin both health and happiness for want of a friendly hand. She felt as though he had appealed to her for help, and she had tacitly refused it. It was surely in the highest degree improbable that she could be of the slightest use to him; yet was it not her duty to try? Was conventionality to be put before even the faintest chance of helping a fellow-creature? The thought of the widowed mother decided her to cast prudence to the winds, and yield to a generous impulse.

"I don't know whether you would care to come in here sometimes in the evening?" she said hesitatingly. "I am nearly always at home, except on Mondays, and if you would come without waiting for a special invitation, I should be very pleased to see you. I am afraid you would find it rather dull; but I could show you some exercises with the clubs, and play the accompaniments, though I am not much of a musician."

"Now, I do call that kind!" he cried, his face lighting up. "I shall like it of all things, and I only hope you won't find that I take you too literally at your word. But you must promise to turn me out if I bore you too often."

"Then it's a bargain," said Candida, inwardly wondering how far the mild entertainment which she had to offer would be able to compete with the charms of whisky, poker, and music-hall artistes.

CHAPTER X.

ONE afternoon, some three or four months later, as the two girls were sitting together at tea, a large cardboard box was brought in, addressed to Miss St. John.

"What's that?" asked Sabina. "You don't mean to say that you have been buying a new hat all of your own accord?"

Candida looked slightly embarrassed.

"My winter hat is getting so very shabby," she said apologetically; "and you are always telling me how unbecoming it is, and what a fright I look in it. But, as you know, I am a perfect baby in the hands of those alarmingly elegant shopwomen. They bring out all the hideous things that nobody else will buy, jam them on my head, and tell me that I never looked so well in my life."

"You should always take me with you when you go to buy clothes," said Sabina. "Now, let me see what sort of monstrosity you have invested in to-day. H'm, not so bad as usual; there must have been a special providence over you. Come here, and put it on."

Candida knelt down in front of her friend, and submitted to have the broad-leafed black hat placed at different angles upon her head.

"That's better," said Sabina, as she bent the brim into more picturesque curves. "It's really most becoming. It transforms you from a magnificent dowdy into a handsome, stylish-looking woman. How does it suit me?"

She placed the hat on her own curly head, while Candida gazed at her in wistful admiration.

"You always look as pretty as a picture and as smart as paint," she said with a little sigh. "I can't think how you manage it. Now I, except when I am wearing my gymnastic costume, feel as if I had the effect of an anachronism. Fashionable clothes never look natural on me."

"That's because you don't know how to wear them. You've splendid raw material, but you make nothing of it. But why this sudden desire to shine? It would be a dangerous symptom in any other woman."

"I suppose it's natural to wish to look one's best," said Candida. "Circumstances compelled me to be a dowdy for the first year after we came to town, but now there's less occasion for it. And it seems to be considered a woman's first and last duty to look as nice as she can."

"Saul among the prophets," laughed Sabina. "I

shall have to look to my laurels soon. By the way, do you expect your young Adonis to-night? If so, don't ask him to supper, because there's not enough for three."

"I don't suppose he will come to-night," answered Candida. "He has been here twice this week already."

Her anticipation of a solitary evening, however, proved to be unfounded, for about an hour after Sabina had started for the theatre, the bell rang, and Mr. Sylvester was announced.

"I didn't mean to come again so soon," he said apologetically; "but I had nothing to do, and I felt as if I couldn't get through the evening alone. I knew you wouldn't like me to go where I should lose my money, and lay the foundation for a 'head' tomorrow, so here I am."

"I am very glad to see you," said Candida. "You have looked so much better since you took to regular exercise and more regular hours."

"Yes, I'm two inches bigger round the chest already, thanks to Dr. St. John," he said gaily. "And I expect soon to equal Sandow in the matter of muscle. I want you to show me that snake twist with the clubs again to-night, if you don't mind. I couldn't quite get the hang of it last time."

Although nearly four months had passed since Candida had given her impulsive invitation, and though every advantage had been taken of it, she had not yet repented her of her rashness. Sometimes she wondered that she had not tired of the society of her *protégé*, for Adrian, though lively and quick-witted, was but little superior in mind or culture to the average young man of his class. His chief merit was due to the fact that he assumed no pose, made no pretensions to any artistic infallibility, but confessed his ignorance with cheerful unconcern, yawned when he was bored, and positively refused to admire anything that did not really appeal to his taste. His simplicity and naturalness were especially refreshing to one whose chief acquaintance lay among the lesser lights of art and literature, and whose amusement at their affectations had long since changed to weariness and disgust.

But the young man's strongest attraction in the eyes of his girl friend was his habit of consulting her, confiding in her, taking her sympathy for granted, and making her feel that she could be of use to him. Unconsciously, perhaps, she found pleasure in the knowledge that there was some one outside her own family, some one upon whose regard she had no claim of kinship or long habit, who yet honestly admired and appreciated her. Then, too, unlike most young men, he was not in the least afraid of her; he confessed his scrapes to her, laughed at her when she was disposed to be solemn, and made her feel young and foolish again, as she was almost forgetting how to feel under the pressure of work and the burden of responsibility.

Sometimes the pair went out together on Saturday

afternoons to *matinées* or exhibitions, and on these occasions Adrian proved himself a capital playfellow. His spirits were so good, his enjoyment so complete, that Candida usually caught the infection of his gaiety, and gave herself up unreservedly to the pleasure of the moment.

Adrian, in the beginning of their acquaintance, made no attempt to analyze his feelings; he had little turn for analysis of any kind. He only knew that Candida was quite different from any girl of his tolerably numerous acquaintance, and that he admired her more than any of his former loves. Her magnificent health and strength appealed to him the more that he himself was easily tired, and frequently ailing; her calm temperament rested his excitable nerves, and her superiority, so far from humiliating him, only made her friendship the more flattering to his self-love. But the beginning and the end of the whole matter was that he admired her physically, and with him admiration and love were interchangeable terms.

It was not long before he felt that he was desperately in love with this new friend, and that he should never be happy until he had won her for his own; but he was aware that this would only be possible upon terms of marriage, and the idea of marriage had not hitherto found much favour in his eyes. But of late his feelings had been undergoing a gradual change. He was really tired, for the time being, of the monotony of an existence spent between his office, his club, and the music-halls; his mother and sisters were always urging him to marry and settle down, and his doctor had taken to croaking about his health. His income, though a fluctuating one, would allow of his supporting a wife, and from the point of view of family, a Miss St. John of Branksmead would be a brilliant match for him. But to do him justice, such arguments had little weight with him; it was enough that he wanted this girl for his own, and that he could only have her through the gate of marriage.

As yet he had given her no hint of his intentions, for he was not by any means certain of her feeling for him. Being a sceptic as to the possibility of friendship between men and women, he believed that her kindness to himself, and her undisguised liking for his society, were signs that she was, unconsciously perhaps, strongly attracted by him; at the same time, he feared lest by any premature word or deed he should put a stop to their delightful intimacy. A kind of natural instinct, which stands him who possesses it in better stead than wide experience, taught him the best method of treating her, and helped him to steer clear of anything that might frighten or repel her.

To-night, however, he was feeling agitated and uncertain of himself. He had been suffering from "nerves" all day, and at dinner had doctored himself with champagne and liqueurs; but the medicine had failed to effect a cure. He began to wish that he had not come, and to wonder what excuse he could make for an early departure. Meanwhile, he took the clubs in his trembling hands, and Candida sat down to the piano to play an accompaniment to the exercise. As he stood behind her, his attention was distracted by the curve of her neck, and the gleam of the lamplight upon the twisted coils of her hair. His absence of mind resulted in the complete failure of his performance, and the sound of the clubs being knocked awkwardly together made Candida stop playing, and turn round on the stool.

"Oh, you are doing it all wrong," she cried. "I'm afraid you haven't been taking pains. Let me show you again."

She took the clubs from him, tucked up her sleeves, and went through the evolutions of the exercise, while Adrian stood in front of her, his eyes drinking in the exquisite effects produced by the white waving arms, the gleaming ebony clubs, and the unconsciously graceful attitudes. When at length she paused he dared not speak, he scarcely dared to breathe.

"Now," she said, slightly embarrassed in her turn by his silence and strange looks, "let me see you do it without the music. I expect you keep your wrists too stiff."

As she gave him the clubs she started to feel how cold his hands were. Thinking that he must be ill, she glanced anxiously in his face, and saw that his cheeks were flushed and his eyes burning.

"You are so beautiful to-night!" he said under his breath.

Involuntarily Candida stepped backwards, a startled look coming into her face. Her movement of suggested flight, the unwonted timidity of her expression gave him a sudden spurt of courage. The clubs fell to the ground with a crash as he sprang forward and threw himself at her feet.

"I love you!" he cried, almost grovelling before her—"I love you! No, don't push me away; don't be unkind to me. For Cod's sake say you love me too! You must; you belong to me. Nobody ever loved you as I do."

"Oh, don't—please don't!" exclaimed Candida, astonished to find that all her boasted self-possession had deserted her. "I would so much rather you didn't. Oh, do get up; please let me go."

Was that little trembling, imploring voice really her own? Was this foolish, shrinking, breathless creature really her calm and dignified self? What strange magic could have been laid upon her that she was thus transformed in a moment into an awkward frightened girl, without even the strength of mind to deal with an undesired avowal? She told herself angrily that she must throw off this weakness, must put a stop to this dreadful scene. With a determined effort she freed herself from her lover's clasp, and retreated behind the table. But in an instant he was by her side, was leaning over her, was looking imploringly into her face.

"You have always been so kind to me," he murmured. "Don't be cruel to me now. Make me happy just for this one evening; say you love me, whether you do or not. No, don't take your hands away; don't drive me from you. Be good to me, darling! We have been so happy together; why shouldn't we be together always?"

Candida put her hand up to her throat. She was feeling as if two forces were at war within her. Her will, her reason remained firm and inflexible, but her senses were in open rebellion, were fighting wildly for freedom. Even her nerves and muscles seemed to be in league with the enemy, for her arms were struggling to throw themselves around the petitioner at her side, and her fingers were tingling to twine themselves in his. A sudden sensation of intense languor overcame her; she felt an almost irresistible impulse to lay her head upon her lover's shoulder, and shed tears of sheer exhaustion. In mortal terror lest her will should give way beneath the strain, she stood stiffly upright, and forced herself to speak.

"Pray don't talk like that," she said, trying to speak naturally. "This is all a mistake, a delusion. We are friends and comrades, nothing more; it is absurd to suppose that we ever could be more. You are not yourself to-night; you have been carried away by some passing fancy. To-morrow you will be ready to laugh at yourself for thinking that we were suited to each other; you will realize that you would tire of me in a month. Then you will thank me for not having taken you *au sérieux*, and we shall soon be as good friends as ever."

"Now you are cruel," broke in Adrian, vehemently. "I did not think you could be so hard, so untrue to yourself and me. Why, ever since I have known you, you have been the only woman in the world for me; the others have all seemed like mere shadows by the side of you. And how dare you say that we are not suited to each other, that I should tire of you in a month? You won't let your own heart speak, and you stop your ears against the pleadings of mine. Yet I believe," he went on in softer tones, "I feel—yes, I *know*—that you are beginning to love me. You told me so yourself when you were silent; it is only your lips that deny it. I thought you prided yourself on your honesty? Oh, my dearest, why won't you tell me the truth? Why won't you say you love me? I am so tired of being alone, and so hungry for love."

His voice broke, and Candida perceived, with a great pang at her heart, that the tears were standing in his dark eyes. He had come so close to her that she could feel his breath upon her cheek; but she was unable to move, though she knew that his arm was stealing gently round her. She made no effort to free herself, though as she noticed his dawning smile of triumph she longed to strike him on the mouth. But instead she closed her eyes, and was conscious that for a moment their lips met. Then, as though the spell were broken, she tore herself away from him, and sprang to the other side of the room.

"Oh, what *are* we doing?" she cried, putting her hands to her head. "What must you think of me? I suppose this is all my fault. I do beg your pardon for letting you kiss me; but indeed I didn't intend to. I must have been mad. I don't want to hurt you, but you mustn't think that I love you, or can ever marry you. I know I've behaved very badly, but I hope you'll forgive me in time."

There was no mistaking the sincerity of her tone, and the triumphant lover of a moment before was instantly sobered.

"Do you mean that?" he asked, looking as though he could scarcely believe his ears. "You have been leading me on like any society coquette, encouraging me to make a fool of myself, and now you turn round and say you did not mean anything—you were only playing with me!"

"No, no, I wasn't playing; I don't know what I was doing," cried Candida in an agony of remorse. "I only know that I have always liked you very much, and enjoyed laughing and talking to you; but that is not love. So, though I shall miss you very much, I think we ought not to meet for some time, not until you have forgotten all this folly, and can look upon me as a friend again."

"If you send me away from you like this," said Adrian, white with anger and wounded vanity, "I shall never come back again. You may call my love folly, but it is serious enough to me; and, though I may be only good to laugh and talk with, I can suffer as much as any of your solemn prigs. Good-bye," he added, with a sudden change of tone. "I dare say you are quite right to send me about my business. Don't make yourself unhappy about me. I was a presumptuous ass to think you could ever care for me."

In another moment he was gone, and Candida drew a deep sigh of relief as she heard the front door bang; yet mingled with her relief was a faint dull sense of disappointment. The victory was hers, but it was the type of victory that is only less disastrous than defeat. She had been obliged to hold her heart in both hands, and even then she had felt it slipping through her fingers. With a keen sense of humiliation she recalled her momentary surrender. How could it have happened? she asked herself again and again, for all the while her will had never wavered, and the voice of reason had argued so convincingly against the pleadings of her lover.

And now another new and unwelcome experience befell her. Instead of falling, almost as soon as her head touched the pillow, into an untroubled, dreamless sleep, she tossed restlessly to and fro during wakeful, feverish hours, tormented by conflicting thoughts and desires, with now and again a lapse into unconsciousness, from which she awoke with the sensation of a touch upon her lips, and the close pressure of arms about her waist. And each awaking to reality was accompanied by some feeling that strangely resembled loss and disillusionment. When morning came her eyes were sore, her head aching, her whole frame exhausted and unstrung. Yet she rejoiced to see the dawn, for now she could throw off the harassing visions of the night, and find forgetfulness in her work.

Her work! The very thought of it filled her with fresh courage and vigour. How she pitied other girls who were forced to eat out their hearts in idleness, to dance and dress and smile and chatter, hiding their haggard looks beneath "face joy," the costliest mask that women wear. For herself, she felt convinced that her peace of mind would soon be regained. She had been incredibly weak and foolish, but at last she had perceived the precipice to whose brink she had strayed, and she had drawn back in time. She would look back upon this little incident in later days as one of the lessons of life—a valuable experience, no doubt, but still a thing apart, a mere episode, certainly not "her whole existence."

CHAPTER XI.

IN spite of all her courage and determination, in spite of all her resources in the shape of work and study, Candida was no less surprised than annoyed at the sense of blank and loneliness which the loss of her late constant companion left in her life. Before she had known him solitude had possessed no terrors for her; as long as she was seeing him continually she had not consciously set a high value upon his society. But now, as she recognized with self-contempt, her egoism or her vanity hungered for the subtle flattery with which he alone had fed it. She missed the admiring eyes, the sympathetic manners, the boyish confidences, the light-hearted irresponsible talk and laughter to which she had become accustomed during the past few months. Books seemed for the time being to have lost their savour, and the visits to concerts or theatres, which when shared had been so full of interest and enjoyment, now appeared insufferably dull and tiresome. Memories of that brief period of bright companionship were associated with certain of the streets, the railway stations and the shops. At that corner of Oxford Street Adrian had bought her a bunch of violets, paying double the price demanded for it. Although the flower-girl had deserted the spot, the perfume of violets lingered about it still. At this confectioner's in the Strand they had more than once had tea together. Why should it seem so different from all other shops?

There were moments when she felt almost irresistibly impelled to write to him, and beg him to come back upon the old terms; moments when some invisible power seemed to be drawing her feet towards the neighbourhood in which he lodged, or the streets through which he walked on his way home from the office; moments when the sight of a handsome, pale-faced, dark-eyed youth advancing towards her sent the blood to her cheek, and made all her pulses throb.

How absurd it all was, she would tell herself angrily, for in spite of these suspicious symptoms she was not in love with Adrian; certainly she had no desire to marry him. She was convinced that he was thoroughly unsuited to domestic life; the very idea of him in the *rôle* of householder and paterfamilias was hopelessly ludicrous. No, he was an agreeable companion and fair-weather friend, but not a man in whom it was possible to place implicit confidence, certainly not a mate for life.

As the weeks passed on, the feeling of loss and loneliness began gradually to fade away. The holidays were drawing near, and she looked forward eagerly to the summer months that would be spent among her own people in her own home. She would have her father for a companion there, to say nothing of Ted Ferrars, who was by no means to be despised. She had seen very little of Ted for some time past; when he was not on circuit, he was working so hard in town that he found it necessary to spend most of his Sundays in the country boating, or playing golf. She felt convinced that he had long since forgotten his old foolish fancy for herself, and now they would be as good friends as ever.

Her spirits began to recover their former serenity now that she felt free and at ease in her mind again. Many girls, she reflected with self-congratulation, would have mistaken her sensations for love, and shipwrecked their lives on the rock of that error. People were so apt to forget that there were a thousand imitations of the one and only love. What she had experienced had been one of the imitations, a mere Brummagem article, from which the plating had quickly worn, and displayed the baser metal beneath.

Returning home from her work one June afternoon, Candida found a letter awaiting her, addressed in an unknown hand. The first glance at its contents destroyed in one blow the shelter of complacent indifference that she had so carefully built up for her perturbed spirit. After the opening sentence the words swam before her eyes, and a deadly chill settled upon her heart.

The letter was signed "Margaret Sylvester," and the writer stated that her son Adrian had been dangerously ill from inflammation of the lungs, accompanied by severe nervous prostration, brought on, it was supposed, by overwork and exposure. Although rather better, he was still so weak that the doctor did not yet consider him out of danger. In his delirium Miss St. John's name had been constantly on his lips, and now that he was sensible again, he had begged that she might be asked to come and see him, perhaps for the last time.

"Exposure and overwork!" Candida could guess what that meant. It was her cruelty that had driven him to recklessness and despair. She had been so anxious to save her own soul, to guard her own happiness, that she had spared no thought for him. Poor fellow, what had she done to him? Even now he might die, and then she would have murdered him. A flood of pity and tenderness filled her heart as she remembered his bright boyish ways, his light-hearted laugh, his absolute devotion to herself. And now to think of him lying there, pale and weak and wasted by sickness, all for love of her. It was like an episode out of some ancient tale of chivalric romance. If he were ready to die for her, surely the least she could do would be to live for him. No one had ever loved her as he did; probably no one ever would again.

While these thoughts passed through her mind she was already on her way to Doughty Street, where Adrian lodged. Presently, as though in a sort of dream, she found herself being received by a little grey-haired lady with a soft voice and anxious expression, and ushered into a room where lay a pale, hollow-cheeked youth, who gazed at her wistfully out of sunken eyes.

"Have you really come?" he murmured feebly, "or have I got the fever again? I have seen you every night since I was ill, but you never spoke, and always melted away when I tried to touch you. Is it really you?"

"Yes, it is really I," she said, kneeling down beside the bed, and taking his thin hand in hers. "I'm not going to melt away this time. My poor boy, what have you been doing to yourself? Why didn't you let me know that you were ill before?"

"I—I didn't like to bother you," he returned. "I didn't think that you would care."

Candida put her mouth close to his ear.

"Was it all my fault?" she whispered.

"No, no, you mustn't think that," he answered in the same tone. "You couldn't help not caring about me; I ought never to have expected it. Only, when I knew I had lost you, I felt as if nothing really mattered, and I went and played the fool rather more than usual. I caught a bad chill on the top of it all, and—and here I am. I've lost all my muscle again," he concluded ruefully.

"I was a selfish, cold-blooded prig," she said remorsefully. "I did care about you all the time. At least, I had begun to, but I wouldn't let myself go on. I did my best to stamp out my tender feeling for you, because I was afraid that it would not lead to my own happiness; I never gave a thought to yours. Forgive me, dear. Get better as fast as you can, and when the holidays begin we will go down to Branksmead together, and I will nurse you back to health and strength again."

He looked up at her with the trustful smile of a sick child.

"I can hardly believe my own happiness," he said. "I thought that I had lost you, and was going to die, and now you and life have come back to me together."

The tears of weakness began to trickle down his cheeks, but Candida took out her handkerchief and wiped them away. Then, not being a woman who did things by halves, she bent down and kissed him.

"I will come and see you again to-morrow," she said. "But I must not stay longer now, or I shall tire you out."

Mrs. Sylvester, who had been waiting outside the sick-room, accompanied her visitor down the stairs.

"Did you think him looking very ill?" she asked.

There was a flicker of interest and curiosity in her sad eyes as they rested on the stranger's handsome face.

"Yes, but I am sure he will get better very quickly now," answered Candida. "And then he must have a long holiday in the country. You won't mind my coming to see him again to-morrow, will you?"

"Mind!" repeated the other. "Why, it will do him more good than all the doctors in London. Of course, it's easy to see that he worships the ground you walk on. Poor boy! all he wants is some nice girl to care for him, and take an interest in him. They say that good sons make good husbands, and though Adrian may have his faults, he has been the best of sons to me, always kind and thoughtful and considerate."

Candida, in considerable embarrassment, stammered that she was delighted to hear it, and then hastily made her escape.

Thanks to the new hope and happiness that had come into his life, the invalid made rapid progress, and by the time the holidays began, though still weak, he was able to travel down to Branksmead, escorted by Candida, who had received her father's permission to bring an invalid friend. Leaning upon her arm, Adrian entered the hall, where he was taken possession of by Mrs. St. John and her sister-in-law, whose hearts were instantly won by his good looks and evident delicacy.

During the first few days of his stay the guest

was regarded in all good faith as an interesting young *protégé* of Candida's, and she herself was not quite clear as to what really were the relations that existed between them, until, as Adrian's strength returned, he gave her to understand both by words and looks that he depended upon her keeping the compact that had been implied rather than spoken by his bedside. He evidently regarded himself as her accepted lover, and though she had her fears as to the future which might be in store for her as his wife, she was unable, and indeed unwilling, to draw back from the position which she had taken up.

It was not long before Mr. St. John began to have his doubts as to the disinterestedness of his daughter's conduct. He had intercepted stolen glances which roused his suspicions, and overheard half-uttered words which went near to confirming them; for during those long sunny days the undeclared lovers were going through a second period of courtship, and were apt to forget that they were not the only inhabitants of their summer paradise.

"That young friend of yours is a very pretty fellow," remarked the squire one day, when he found himself alone with his daughter. "He has pretty manners, too, and a pretty touch on the piano. He reminds me of an Arcadian shepherd who has strayed to town, and exchanged some of his Arcadian simplicity for the customs of the city. Those premature crowsfeet contrast so oddly with his boyish air and otherwise youthful appearance."

"He is not really so very juvenile," said Candida, looking rather disturbed. "I think he is nearly thirty, but people always fancy that he is much younger than his years."

"A sign of an irresponsible nature," observed her father. "I wonder whether the shakiness of his hand is due entirely to his late illness? He seems thoroughly to appreciate your grandfather's old Madeira."

His daughter turned on him indignantly.

"Do you grudge it to him?" she demanded. "I brought him here, weak and ill as he was, because I thought that he would meet with kindness and welcome. I would never have done so if I had known that he would be grudged food and drink, and that his weakness would only be laughed at."

"My dear girl, what is all this about?" asked the squire, in amazement. "I grudge your young friend nothing, not even the Madeira. But apparently you object to my criticizing him, even in fun. Is he copyright, or have you taken out a patent for him?"

"I don't like you to laugh at him," replied Candida, turning aside her head. "It—it hurts me."

"And pray why should it do that? What possible interest can you feel in this agreeable youth beyond that of friendly kindness?"

"That's just what I have been wanting to tell you, only it seemed impossible as long as nothing was definitely settled. I have agreed to marry him if he still wishes it when he is quite strong again."

Her father threw up his hands with a gesture of despair, and strode to the other end of the room without a word.

"It's all over with you," he said at length, coming back and standing in front of her. "It's all over with you if you adhere to that decision. You poor dear simpleton, you great stupid baby, do you know what you are doing? You, whom I have hitherto regarded as a girl of some sense and judgment, you contemplate throwing yourself away on this dissipated young whippersnapper, who is a mere bundle of nerves and emotions, who would tire of you or any woman in three months, who is in a fair way to wear himself out before he is forty! You are not in the habit of joking, but I hope that for once you are amusing yourself at my expense."

"No, I am perfectly serious," replied his daughter. "But I can thoroughly enter into your feelings on the subject, because I felt very much the same myself only a few weeks ago. I cannot explain all the reasons that have made me change my mind—probably you would not understand them if I did—but the conclusion of the whole matter is that Adrian loves me, and thinks, rightly or wrongly, that his happiness and well-being depend on me; and that I—well, I suppose that I love him too, for I only desire to be good to him, and make him happy."

"Love!" cried her father, contemptuously. "I don't believe you know the meaning of the word. You are carried away by a passing fancy for the *beaux yeux* of this young puppy, just as a man is often possessed by a temporary infatuation for a pretty face, and you, no more than he, pause to ask if there is anything behind it. If you marry this grown-up boy, what, in heaven's name, is to become of you when your youth and his are past? How can you settle down as companions for life when you have scarcely an idea or an interest in common? It is bad enough for an intelligent man to be tied to a pretty face with nothing behind it, but it is infinitely worse for a woman, more particularly a woman like you."

"I think you are unjust to Adrian," said Candida, keeping her temper by a strong effort. "He may not be exactly intellectual, but he is quick and intelligent, and has a natural taste for art. One doesn't marry a man in order to discuss abstract questions with him." She paused for a moment, and then went on with a visible effort. "And as for love, you must remember that love does not always grow up just when and where it ought, or depend altogether upon similarity of ideas and community of tastes. All I know is, that up to within the last few months I used to pass the lovers in the streets and parks, and wonder what magic it could be that made their dull, tired faces so radiant when they were together, and why they looked so happy as long as their hands were clasped, even though they seldom exchanged a word. They seemed to have learnt some wonderful secret to which I had no clue. I should have despised them, perhaps, if I had not guessed that there must be something more than mere sentimental folly in a phase of mind through which, at one time or another, the whole of humanity seems to pass. I have learnt their secret now. What right have I to refuse myself to the man who has opened my eyes to the greatest mystery of life, more especially when that man claims my help, looks to me for strength and support?"

"What right have you to wreck your own happiness by throwing yourself away upon a man who is unworthy of you?"

"Happiness!" cried Candida, in supreme contempt. "There is no such thing as happiness, permanent happiness, except for children and fools. No grown-up thinking person ever achieves happiness, least of all a woman. The people who come nearest to happiness are those who do their best to throw it away, the women who devote their lives to the sick and the sorry, the outcast and despised. Nobody thinks them foolish or misguided, though they are only actuated by an impersonal desire to help their fellows, and be of use in their generation. Why should not I devote myself to the man I love, without considering the possible risk to my own happiness?"

"Because marriage, unlike philanthropy, cannot be renounced if you find it a failure. However, I have neither the right nor the power to coerce you in this matter. I have always held that men and women should be free to follow their own inclinations in marriage, and that their parents and guardians should refrain from all interference; but it is sometimes very hard to act up to one's theories. I will take an early opportunity of having a confidential talk with this—with your—with Mr. Sylvester, and perhaps I may find that I have taken too gloomy a view of himself and his circumstances."

"I don't think you will," said Candida, frankly. "I doubt if a more unsatisfactory match could be found from the common-sense point of view. Dear father, I am so sorry to be such a disappointment to you, after all the trouble you have taken about me. Don't think I can ever forget how much I owe you. I may make shipwreck of my life, but, thanks to you, I shall always be able to build a raft."

CHAPTER XII.

SHORTLY after Candida's engagement was made known to her family, Ted Ferrars arrived at the Vicarage. Ted already had his suspicions that something was going wrong with his course of true love, and now those suspicions were only too thoroughly confirmed. While he had been working early and late with the object of providing a home at no very distant date for the girl he loved, working so incessantly that he could allow himself but little of her society in the present, this impudent, worthless, curly-headed puppy had stepped in and carried off the prize. At first he felt it almost impossible to realize that the chief object of his life had been destroyed at one blow, that the reward which was to crown all his endeavours, his other self, whose image had occupied his heart for years past, whom he had hoped to gain for his own in the years to come, had been snatched from him by this stranger, leaving him forlorn and destitute, without purpose in the present, without hope for the future. The wound in his heart was too deep to cause him as yet more than a dull, though chronic, ache, but the wound to his vanity pained him acutely, so that it was natural he should cast about him for some means to heal the smart.

Sabina had lately arrived at the Hall, and finding herself occupying the unusual position of "odd woman out," was already in the first throes of depression and ennui. Candida, she thought, had behaved rather badly in pretending to be indifferent to men and marriage, and then throwing herself into the arms of the first good-looking youth who had made love to her. It was very hard, she complained, to have to give up her friend and housemate to a man who was so obviously unworthy of her; she had really never expected that Candida would act with so little sense or discrimination. Some of these sentiments she confided to Ted, who received them with approbation, and confessed to his complete agreement with them. He admitted to himself that he had wronged Sabina hitherto in regarding her as a silly, empty-headed little flirt, for she really seemed to have a good deal of sense and a very just perception of character. He had never before realized the unusual charm of her manner, and her beauty was undeniable. Most fellows would think themselves uncommonly lucky to enjoy long uninterrupted *tête-à-têtes* with her. In short, Sabina's society, her gracious smiles and her appealing glances, constituted the most healing treatment for the wound that had been dealt to his self-love, even though they had no power to soothe or satisfy his heart.

Meanwhile, Mr. St. John had been studying his daughter's *fiancé* with closer attention, and on more than one occasion had succeeded in inveigling the young man, despite all his efforts to escape, into the study for confidential conversation. These interviews left him no better satisfied than before with the prospects of the match.

"I have been cross-examining Mr. Sylvester on the subject of his worldly affairs," he told his daughter one day. "The income upon which he proposes to marry and found a family seems to be charmingly precarious. As far as I can make out, he has a hundred or two a year of his own, and is in partnership with some other scatter-brained young fellow as stockbrokers or stock-jobbers, or something of the kind. Altogether, he can reckon, he assures me, upon an average of seven or eight hundred a year. What a shocking life for an active young fellow! He'd be much better employed in chopping wood."

"I am not in the least afraid of poverty," said Candida. "We are to live with his mother at first, because she has a very small income, and Adrian says it will be a help to her to have us to board with her, as he won't be able to make her an allowance after he is married. He is devoted to his mother, and she to him."

"*Ma mère!* Yes, a most effective allusion on the stage, or in a French murder trial."

"Now you are unjust to him," cried Candida, with some warmth. "Why should he pretend to be fond of his mother? Most young men pretend to be ashamed of theirs. But the fact is, you don't like him, and so you refuse to see any good in him."

"No, I don't like him," returned her father. "I don't like his face, though I admit that it is absurdly handsome, and I don't like his soft voice or his pretty manners. I don't like the shakiness of his hand, nor the lines round his eyes, nor the fact that he never looks at me when I am speaking to him. I imagine that he has a tolerably intimate acquaintance with life as it is lived by young men about town."

"I don't suppose he has been a saint," said Candida, with a quick flush. "I know he is weak—perhaps he has been wicked; but in that case he has all the more need of pity and help."

"On the same principle, I suppose, that charitable ladies assist the drunken loafer who flaunts his rags in their faces, while the 'deserving poor' are left to look after themselves."

Candida was silent for a moment. She could scarcely remember any subject upon which she and her father had not been of the same mind, and it hurt her keenly that upon this, the most important decision of her whole life, they should be so completely at variance.

"Mother is pleased at my engagement," she said at length. "And so is Aunt Aggie. They were afraid that I should never marry."

"And women think a disastrous marriage better than none at all," he retorted. "Well, I suppose your mind is made up. You are yet another victim to that foolish craving for self-sacrifice which the teaching of centuries has implanted in the feminine breast. But I confess that I am disappointed in you, Candida. I see that a masculine education doesn't hinder a woman from making a fool of herself about some man."

Candida went and knelt down beside his chair.

"Dear father," she said softly, "does a masculine education ever hinder a man from making a fool of himself about some woman?"

In spite of Mr. St. John's disapproval, the lovers were very happy together during those summer weeks. Adrian was naturally of an ardent and susceptible disposition, and he honestly believed himself to be in love for the first and last time. Candida, being really a novice in the tender passion, was almost carried off her feet by the adoration of which she found herself the object, and was no less flattered than bewildered by her lover's unwillingness to let her out of his sight, and the fact that he seemed to have no eyes or ears for any one else as long as she was by his side.

The date of the marriage was a vexed question

Mr. St. John wished it to be put off for a year, at least, Adrian pleaded that it might take place as soon as possible after their return to town, while Candida herself desired to fix it for a day early in January, in order that she might give her employer three months' notice. Ultimately her wishes were allowed to prevail, although Mr. St. John only gave in on condition that his daughter consented to accept the small allowance for dress and pocket-money that she had hitherto refused.

Autumn came too soon for each member of the party. Even Sabina, who cared little for the country, had grown interested in the task she had set herself of subjugating the unsuspecting Ted. Sabina was a creature to whom friendship with a member of the opposite sex was a physical impossibility. As she grew more intimate with the disconsolate young man, her latent coquetry awoke, and from sheer force of habit she began to put forth all her wiles to lure him into her net.

Ted, unconscious of what was happening to him, became more than ever convinced of Miss Romney's beauty and charm, and began to have a dim suspicion that she appreciated his own character and society. Though she was always ready to talk enthusiastically about Candida, and condole with him upon his disappointment, yet the conversation had a curious knack of coming round to their own personalities, and the peculiar traits in their characters. She seemed such a timid, trustful little creature that Ted was convinced that the stage was a most unsuitable profession for her, and decided that somebody—he did not quite know whom—ought to take care of her, and provide her with all the comforts and luxuries of life.

Perhaps his feeling for her would never have advanced beyond a kindly interest if his cousin and old schoolmate, Captain James Ferrars, had not come to spend the last fortnight of the holidays at the Rectory. Captain Jim conceived a sudden and enthusiastic admiration for Miss Romney, constituted himself her shadow, and succeeded in involving her in one of the violent flirtations for which Ted remembered that he was famous in his regiment. Coarse brute! The fact that the poor child was on the stage was quite enough to make him take advantage of her innocence, and do his best to break her heart. But if he had any designs against her peace of mind, he should find that he had some one else to reckon with, some one who was ready to play the part of a brother to her. Alas, for poor human nature! Sabina's beauty and fascination increased a thousandfold in Ted's eyes, now that she was monopolized by another man.

The day before that on which the party at Branksmead was to break up, Ted, having seen his cousin off at the station, went up to the Hall, where he found Sabina sitting alone in the garden. There was something pensive, almost disconsolate, in her attitude.

Could she, he wondered, be regretting the departure of her late admirer?

"I suppose you'll be delighted to turn your back on the country to-morrow," he said abruptly, as he seated himself beside her. "This must seem a fearfully dull hole to you, after all the excitements of town."

"Ah, you are evidently no thought-reader," she answered, turning eyes upon him so softly bright that he instantly repented himself of his *brusquerie*. "I was just wishing that I could have this summer over again; it has been such a happy time. I shall feel so lonely when I get back to town. Of course, Candida will have no time to waste on me, and somehow one sees so little of one's real friends in London."

"You will let me come and see you sometimes?" he put in. "We are real friends now, aren't we?"

"Oh, I hope so," she said, dropping her eyes. "Will you come and see me, even after Candida is married? I shall have to chum up with another girl, I suppose, and most of them are such cats. I shall never find another like her."

"No, there is nobody like her," he agreed, loyally echoing her sigh. "But I hope you won't think me impertinent if I say that I wish you could find an older friend to live with. You are so much too—too young and pretty to set up with a girl of your own age. You ought to have some one to take care of you. You see, I am giving myself the privileges of an old friend."

"It is so good of you to care—to take any interest in my fate," she said, with a pathetic note in her voice. "It seems quite wonderful to me, because I have had no one to take care of me for three years, no one to whom it mattered whether I were alive or dead. And—and I always thought you regarded me as a mere frivolous little doll, quite unworthy of the friendship of any sensible man."

She smiled at him as she spoke, but he fancied that a tear was trembling on the end of her long lashes. It was strange what magic power could be contained in one little tear-drop; it seemed to scald his heart and brain. A sudden longing came over him to seize her in his arms, and kiss away that tear. The next moment he told himself that he was a brute, and pictured to himself the horror that would overwhelm his gentle companion could she but guess the thoughts and impulses that were passing through his mind. But he could and would control himself. He had nothing to offer this poor pretty child, no love, no home, and to pretend to make love to her under those circumstances would be a cowardly insult, the more so since he knew that she had no natural protector to call him to account.

With a mighty effort he turned away his eyes from the lovely mournful face, and, gripping the bench with his would-be rebel arms, answered in as steady a voice as he could assume—

"And I always thought you regarded me as a dull,

heavy sort of fellow, quite beneath the notice of a triumphant young beauty. Perhaps we misjudged each other. Anyway, please don't say again that there is no one who takes any interest in your fate, or cares whether you are alive or dead. That is rather cruel to your friends, and I can't allow it now that I am admitted among the number."

Sabina looked round at him in surprise. Long practice in the art of flirtation, and unusual sensitiveness to the mental temperature of her admirers, had led her fully to expect an avowal of some kind at this juncture. That a man should keep his head when she had arranged that he should lose it, and resist a temptation that she had placed in his way, was so great a novelty in her experience that she was startled into naturalness and sincerity.

"You are very kind and good," she said frankly. "And it will mean more to me than you can guess to feel that I have one real honest friend among all the indifferent acquaintances and pretended admirers who only seek me as long as I can amuse them, and who would drop me to-morrow if I lost my looks, or were ill and out of spirits. You are different from all the others. I believe I can trust you."

Again the desire to give this dangerously fascinating friend some tangible proof of his regard swept over the young man. Fearful lest he should disgrace himself for ever in her eyes, he sprang to his feet, and, muttering an incoherent hope that he might be allowed

THE CAREER OF CANDIDA.

to serve her should occasion ever arise, he sought safety in flight, leaving Sabina still seated on the bench, with an unusually thoughtful expression upon her pretty face.

* * * * *

The Piccadilly Theatre opened that autumn with a new "comedy farce" which, it was supposed, would appeal to all classes of playgoers, but which, as events proved, was of the kind that only appeals to the class that never pays for its seats. The deadhead, who is notoriously hard to please, approved of the play, and attended regularly, but the paying public stayed away. So it came about that at the end of three weeks the piece, upon the mounting of which an unusually large sum had been spent, was withdrawn, and the theatre was sub-let to an actor-author-manager who was anxious to produce a romantic drama of his own composition. This drama, having nothing in common with real life, proved a prodigious success, being played to crowded houses for five hundred nights. But, alas! there was no part in the new piece for a pretty little actress of the *soubrette* type, and consequently Sabina found herself minus an engagement for the first time in two years.

Thereon followed some weary weeks spent in fruitless visits to agents and managers. Her former good luck had left her quite unprepared for the difficulties which a young and not especially gifted actress who has got "out" often finds in getting "in," and perhaps she was rather hard to please. She objected to boy's parts, and she absolutely refused to go into the provinces, and she would submit to no reduction of salary. She wanted a berth made on purpose for her, said the agents, whose offices were daily besieged by girls who could sing, act, and dance much better than Sabina, and who were willing to do anything and go anywhere. So time passed on, and still Miss Romney was described as "resting," though in point of fact she was employed in the hardest and most unremunerative of all pursuits, that of seeking work and finding none.

Among her friends and acquaintances none was more interested in her search, or sympathized more sincerely in her disappointments, than Ted Ferrars. He called in Blake Street regularly once or twice a week at this time, and as Candida was usually out or otherwise engaged, he enjoyed numerous *tête-à-têtes* with Sabina. The depression of spirits under which she now laboured harmonized with the tone of his own mind far better than her former somewhat flippant gaiety. He still suffered acutely from the disappointment which, he fancied, had blighted his whole existence, and he found his best consolation in the society of another almost equally despondent human being.

Calling in Blake Street late one afternoon, he found Sabina crouching on the hearthrug, the room only lighted by a dull-burning fire. A lamp being brought in directly afterwards, he perceived that her eyes were pink, and that there were traces of tears still upon her cheeks.

"Hasn't the luck turned yet?" he asked kindly. "I hoped you would have heard from Coulson before this."

"No, I'm afraid he's a base deceiver, like all the rest," answered Sabina, turning her face away from the light. "I see the rehearsals have already begun at the Pall Mall. I don't believe I shall ever get another engagement. Can you tell me which is the most luxurious workhouse in London? I should like one of those where Sundays out are allowed, and where they have dramatic entertainments at Christmas. One is always reading paragraphs in the newspapers about the way in which the able-bodied paupers are pampered."

"Ah, it's all very well for you to make light of it now," he said. "That is only to put me off the scent. You were crying when I came into the room."

"And why shouldn't I cry if I like?" she demanded, with sudden warmth. "I suppose even able-bodied paupers are allowed the luxury of tears? And I wasn't joking, either; I have only five pounds between me and the workhouse. Of course, I ought to have saved; Candida was always worrying me about it, but somehow the money slipped away."

"Of course it did," he returned sympathetically.

"You were never meant to bother your head with money, or any such prosaic details. Girls like you ought always to have some one to take care of them, and work for them, so that they may be left free to enjoy all the gladness of life."

Sabina sighed, but made no answer, and for some moments silence reigned between them. Ted thought that he had never seen her look so soft, so sweet, so innocent as she did at that moment, with her ruffled hair, drooping mouth, and eyes still misty with tears. She was sad and lonely, like himself; would it not be possible for them to console each other? Though he had lost the woman who was all the world to him, might he not find comfort in the love of another, and win back his own happiness by providing for hers? Certain it was that his dreary purposeless existence had become almost intolerable, and the void in his heart was crying out to be filled. He felt sure that he was not disagreeable to this girl; she already liked and trusted him as a friend, surely it would not be very hard to win her. In imagination he could see her happy and at peace in the nest that he would build for her, loving him with the blind, unquestioning devotion that only such women knew how to give, welcoming him on every home-coming with eyes that always brightened, and lips that always smiled, and arms that were always open for him alone. The image of the comrade-wife that had so long occupied his heart grew dim before the vision of this clinging, melting, helpless, feminine presence that would brood over his home, and fill the dreary rooms with warmth and light.

"I wish—I wish that you would let me take care of you in future," he murmured. "Will you, dearest? Could you trust yourself to me?"

He tried to take her hand, but she pulled it sharply away.

"You are only saying that out of pity," she cried. "You don't love me a bit, really."

"Pity for myself, then," he returned, seizing her hand again. "Will you take care of me? You don't know how badly I want it. I can't swear that you are my first and only love, but if you will only take me as I am, and give me a little sympathy, a little tenderness, I will repay you with all my devotion in the years to come. My only thought shall be to make you happy, to shield you from all trouble and sorrow. Say you will try and love me a little—say yes, darling."

Sabina was silent for a moment.

"I wish I could—I wish I could," she said at length, with a ring of regret in her voice. "If only it were possible!"

"But it *is* possible," he cried, slipping his arm round her waist. "You beautiful darling, I believe you do care just a little for me, though I can't imagine why you should. Do you—do you—just the least little bit? If so, nothing shall ever part us."

For all answer Sabina suddenly burst into tears, and dropped her head upon his shoulder.

"It can't be," she sobbed. "I can never marry you. I shall never marry anybody."

"But, my dearest child," he expostulated, "you must give me some reason for such a determination. Of course, if you don't love me, and think that you never will, that is quite enough; I should never dream of forcing myself upon you. Tell me, is that the reason? You don't like me, you think me ugly and stupid and tiresome, and you don't wish to be bothered by me any more. Say yes, and I'll go away at once, and never trouble you again."

He waited for an answer, but Sabina said nothing, only sobbed more uncontrollably than before.

"You can't say it," he cried triumphantly, wiping away her tears with his pocket-handkerchief. "You can't deny that I have a little corner in your heart. Look up, and tell me that you are going to make me very happy one of these days."

But all the answer he could get from the girl he had thought so soft and yielding was—

"No, no, don't ask me. You don't know. It's quite impossible."

If Sabina had deliberately set herself to fan her wooer's first impulse of chivalrous generosity into something closely resembling genuine passion, she could have chosen no better means than this mingling of regretful tenderness and stubborn resistance. Ted's masculine obstinacy was roused, and though he was considerably puzzled by a decided rejection accompanied by a tacit admission of regard, he concluded that this was but an exhibition of girlish coyness or timidity, and that he had only to exercise a little tact and patience in order to gain his ends. A ring at the bell caused Sabina to spring from his side, and run to her room before he could obtain any explanation of her mysterious conduct, but he departed with the inward determination of giving her no peace until she had either promised to make him happy, or else convinced him that there was some good reason for her refusal.

CHAPTER XIII.

IT must not be supposed that Candida was too much absorbed in her own love-affair to be oblivious of the little romance that was being enacted at her elbow, nor can it be asserted that she was free from all feeling of pique when she perceived the ease and rapidity with which a once-devoted lover was able to transfer his affections. Yet another proof, she reflected, that men's hearts are tough, and their wounds quickly healed. She took herself to task, however, for this feeling, which was certainly of the dog-in-the-manger order, since she did not want Ted for herself, and therefore had no right to be annoyed at the idea of his marriage with another woman. If he and Sabina really cared for each other she thought that they would be happy together, however ill-assorted such a union might appear in the eyes of the world. Perhaps she had sympathy with ill-assorted couples by reason of the knowledge that her engagement to Adrian was regarded by the whole circle of her acquaintance as hopelessly unsuitable. So she resolved to do all in her power to help forward the affair, which seemed to have stuck fast in a rather inexplicable fashion.

As time passed on, she was surprised at receiving no confidences from her friend, who was unusually silent and subdued in spirit. Could Sabina, she wondered, have turned from Ted's wooing in horror and disgust, as she had turned from that of other men, even when in the first instance she had seemed to be attracted by them?

Candida determined to sound her friend upon the subject as soon as a favourable opening occurred. This opening she thought she had found when, on going into Sabina's room one night to borrow some matches, she found its occupant stretched flat on the floor, with her face hidden in her arms. Candida went and sat down beside her.

"Sabina," she said softly, "something has gone wrong. You are in trouble, and it is a more serious matter than a temporary want of employment. Won't you tell me what it's all about?"

Sabina did not reply at once.

"What is it that they put dogs into when they want to get rid of them painlessly?" she asked at length, in muffled tones. "A lethal chamber, isn't it? I wish some one would put me into a lethal chamber, so that I could have done with it all. I am so tired of being alive."

"Don't talk nonsense," said Candida. "Come, tell

me what is wrong with you; I can guess a certain amount. Ted is in love with you, and you are not altogether indifferent to him, but instead of marrying him like a sensible girl, you prefer to fret yourself to fiddle-strings in solitude. I know you have some prejudice against marriage, and I can understand your shrinking where many men are concerned. But Ted is different; he is kind and considerate and unselfish; he has all the makings of an excellent husband. Let me write to him to-morrow, and tell him that you have changed your mind."

"No, no," cried Sabina, with a shudder, "you don't understand. He doesn't know me. He doesn't really love me; he only loves an ideal of his own creation."

"Well, we can none of us see into each other's hearts," reasoned Candida. "We love or hate people, not for what they really are, but for what they appear to us to be. You have got some strange fancy into your head, or else—or else there is a secret that you have been keeping from me—from us all."

There was no answer, beyond a little moan of despair

"Won't you tell me?" went on Candida, in gentler tones. "Perhaps I might be able to help you. You know that your secret, whatever it is, will be absolutely safe with me."

"I daren't—I daren't," wailed Sabina. "You'd despise me; you'd never speak to me again."

"Oh, how can you say that? Do you think me so hard, so self-righteous? Do trust me, dear. This may be only some trifle that has been magnified by your own fancy."

Candida forced herself to speak hopefully, but a vague fear was pressing like a cold hand upon her heart.

Sabina suddenly raised her head from her arms, and sat upright, a forlorn little figure with wan cheeks and swollen eyes.

"Very well, then, I *will* tell you," she cried recklessly. "I don't care what happens afterwards; I can't keep it to myself any longer. I'm not what you think me; I'm a bad girl. I've committed the one unpardonable sin—in woman. No man would marry me if he knew."

She stopped, and stared at her friend with wide-open, apprehensive eyes, as if she expected a blow, or a word that would be worse than a blow. But Candida drew nearer, and put her arm round the little shrinking figure.

"I have lived with you for three years, and I know you are not a bad girl," she said. "And I don't believe in unpardonable sins. If it won't hurt you, will you tell me what you mean? I suspect that life has been harder for you than I ever guessed."

"I'm afraid you don't understand, even now," said Sabina, mournfully. "I had better tell you the whole story. You remember what I told you about my childhood, how my father deserted us, and my mother slaved to support herself and me."

"Yes, yes," put in Candida, as her friend paused again.

"Well, when I was sixteen she fell ill; I believe it was a break-down from overwork, bad food, and anxiety. I had obtained my first engagement a few months before; it was only a walk-on at a pound a week, but it meant a lot to us. Just when my mother was at her worst, the piece was taken off, and I was told that I shouldn't be wanted for the next one. The morning that I got my dismissal the doctor had told me that unless my mother had plenty of good food, and were kept free from all worry, she could not possibly recover."

"Oh, you poor child!" cried Candida. "What did you do?"

"I was nearly frantic. I adored my mother. I think we were more to each other than most mothers and daughters, because we had gone through so much together, and we were so entirely alone in the world. Of course, I dared not tell her about my dismissal. I took my courage in both hands, and went to the manager. I was horribly afraid of him, though he had always been rather kind to me; but there was something about him that terrified and revolted me. He was a stout, black-bearded man, with protruding eyes and a double chin—a Jew, they said. I had always tried to keep out of his way before, but now I went to him, and told him all our troubles, and implored him to find me something to do in the next piece. He listened to me in silence, staring hard at me all the time out of his dreadful eyes, and when I had finished, he spoke kindly to me, and said he would think it over, and that I was to come and see him again the next morning. I went away full of hope, and the next day he told me that there was a little part in the new piece which he thought I could play, and though he had half promised it to another girl, he felt rather inclined to give it to me. The salary, he said, would be two guineas a week. Oh, Candida, I felt as if I were in heaven; I thought he looked like an angel. I could have gone down on my knees and kissed his feet. He said at last that he would give me the part on one condition, and then—then he told me the condition."

Her voice suddenly failed, and a spasm passed over her face. Candida clasped the trembling form more closely in her arms.

"He said I needn't make up my mind at once; that I could take a day or two to think it over," went on Sabina. "When I left him, I went round to all the agents and managers where I thought I should have the ghost of a chance, but I could hear of nothing. The next day the doctor said my mother must have port wine and turtle soup and jelly and grapes. Unless her strength were kept up, he said she had scarcely a chance of recovery."

There was another halt. Sabina dropped her head on her arms again.

"She had the port wine and things," she muttered. "And she got better, and lived three years longer."

Candida drew a long breath, and then burst into tears.

"You poor darling," she cried passionately, "how I have misjudged you! How you must have suffered! I have sometimes thought you were hard and cynical; I never guessed that you were unhappy. Why didn't you tell me before? I would have been so much kinder to you; I would have tried to make up to you a little for all the martyrdom you have endured."

"I thought you would never speak to me again; that you would utterly despise me," answered Sabina, looking up in surprise, as though she could hardly believe her ears. "If you were like most good women you wouldn't have anything more to do with me."

"No, no," exclaimed Candida. "No woman worthy of the name is hard upon a sister. If she appears to be so, it is because she is coerced by some man—father, brother, or husband."

She stopped abruptly, for her words had brought a new thought into her mind. Sabina seemed to be struck by the same idea.

"Yes, men are always hard upon women," she said. "That's why I refused to marry Ted. I never wanted to marry any one else, though I used to flirt with them; but all the others seemed so horrible and repulsive as soon as they began to make love to me. But Ted never had that dreadful wild-beast look;

he seemed to think more of me than of himself, and to wish to respect me. As you said just now, he was always gentle and considerate, even when he was making love to me. Of course, I might have held my tongue and married him, but, though I know I'm very wicked, I'm not bad enough for that."

"You are not wicked; you have only been the victim of wickedness," said Candida. "But Ted——"

She could not finish her sentence. What would Ted say if he knew all? That was a question which she could not solve with any certainty, though she felt that there ought to be only one answer. Surely no man who professed to love her would turn from this poor little victim who had been sacrificed on the altar of filial love, would not be ready and anxious to console her for the misery of the past, to shield her from all sorrow in the future. But men looked at things so differently from women. She could not tell how Ted, honest, kindly, and chivalrous though he was, would act in such a case as this. Yet she remembered with rising hopes the generous warmth with which he had often inveighed against the unjust hypocritical judgments of the world, and the enthusiasm with which he had espoused the cause of ill-used women and children. Then, too, how often had he quoted with approval passages from poets, moralists, or philosophers, which advocated that equal justice and equal mercy should be extended to the whole race, and that there should be no favouritism on the score of sex.

"Dearest," she said gently, "will you let me tell Ted? You know that your secret would be as safe with him as with me. Let me tell him."

"No, no, I can't," wailed Sabina. "As it is, though he will leave off caring for me in time, he will never have anything but a kindly remembrance of me. I could not bear to know that he despised me, thought of me always with disgust and contempt."

"If he did," cried Candida, "his respect would not be worth having. No, if Ted is what I think him, what he has always appeared to be, he will——" She broke off, fearing lest she had said too much.

Sabina began to cry in feeble, helpless fashion.

"You can do as you please," she sobbed at length. "Tell him, tell everybody; nothing will make any difference. No one will ever love me when they know all about me. Oh, Candida, isn't it hard that if I had told lies at sixteen, or been cruel or mean or treacherous, it would all have been forgotten and forgiven long ago, but this one sin will never be forgotten or forgiven? It has spoilt my whole life."

* * * * *

An evening or two later Ted arrived in Blake Street, in response to a summons from Candida. He wore a cheerful, self-confident air, which was pathetic enough under the circumstances. Candida did her best to tone down his obviously sanguine mood by the gravity of her expression, the solemnity of her greeting. There was an anxious question or two from Ted as to the welfare and whereabouts of Sabina, a reassuring answer from herself, and then, without any circumlocution, she plunged into her painful story. Her hearer was acquainted with the circumstances of Sabina's childhood, but she dwelt upon them for a moment before passing on to the melancholy ending of that childhood. Slowly and brokenly she told her story, while the rare tears overflowed her eyes, and streamed down her cheeks. When she had finished the bare recital of facts she was silent for a moment, half hoping, half expecting that Ted would turn to her with generous ardour, and cry, "Oh, my poor little girl! My love shall make up to her for all the sufferings of the past."

Like Nora, she had expected a miracle to happen, and, like the doll-wife, she was doomed to disappointment. Ted sat silent, staring straight in front of him with set lips and stony eyes.

"Have you nothing to say?" she asked at length.

"I—I'm awfully sorry," he muttered, almost inaudibly.

"Is that all?"

"What can I say?" he returned, stung by her tone. "Poor child, she has been cursedly ill-used; but what can I do? You must understand that this entirely alters the position of things."

Candida made no reply. She dared not take upon

herself the responsibility of influencing his mind, of pleading Sabina's cause.

"God knows I don't judge her, poor little thing!" went on Ted. "I've no right to do that. But this is an awful blow. I dare say you think me a poor-spirited cur, but you know how men look upon these things, and you must admit that it's natural for an old-fashioned fellow like myself to be influenced by the laws and customs of the society in which he finds himself."

"You talk as if our social laws and customs had come down to us from heaven, graven on stone tablets by the finger of God," said Candida, glad to vent her feelings upon an impersonal topic. "But who really makes them, and who enforces them? Not society, not the nation at large, but one small section of it—elderly men. The laws are passed by elderly dried-up statesmen, and interpreted by elderly cynical lawyers, and administered by elderly gouty judges, while the social conventions are enforced by elderly pharisaical citizens, all of them men who have lost their attraction for women, and with it their sympathy for, and understanding of, our sex. What justice or mercy can we look for from such a tribunal?"

"I know that women have had hard measure meted out to them," answered Ted. "I've always said that a man has no right to condemn others for sins that he has committed himself, whatever may have been his excuse; a self-appointed judge is bound to be able to show a clean bill. And I admit that we can't realize women's temptations any more than they can realize ours, so that we have no business to be harder on them than they are on us. But somehow it's deuced hard to put one's theories into practice. One can't help being guided to some extent by the customs and modes of thought that have governed men for centuries. They may be unjust or ill-founded, but you can't expect them to disappear all in a moment. Even if a man knows that he's a low beast himself, he wants his wife to be a superior order of being; he can't bear the notion that other low beasts may fling mud at her. Don't think I really despise that poor child because she has suffered so cruelly. But I can't talk about it now. I must have time to think; I must go away and work it out for myself."

"Yes," said Candida, as she took his hand, "you must work it out for yourself; no one can help you. The answer depends upon the strength of your love, and you alone can tell whether it is strong enough to forgive."

CHAPTER XIV.

A WEEK or ten days passed away before Ted appeared again in Blake Street, and then Candida, on coming home from her work late one afternoon, found him sitting by Sabina's side on the sofa. The young man jumped up, but he did not relinquish his hold of the girl's hand.

"Sabina has consented to make me very happy," he said in rather solemn tones. "I hope you will wish me joy, Candida."

He looked pale and rather worn. It was evident that he had been through a severe struggle, and that he had suffered and made sacrifice before love and pity had been able to win the day.

"I wish you joy with all my heart," cried Candida, as she grasped his hand. "I am so glad! I am sure you will be very happy. We must be married on the same day, Sabina; it will be quite a weight off my mind to know that I am not leaving you alone, after all."

When Ted had taken his departure for the time

being, Sabina launched into an enthusiastic dissertation upon his manifold excellences and her own exceeding good fortune.

"You've no idea how good, how perfectly angelic he was to me," she exclaimed rapturously. "He is so entirely different from all the other men I have ever known. I never thought that any man could be so gentle and considerate, almost reverent. And the engagement-ring is to be one big pearl surrounded by diamonds; he insisted on my telling him what I should like best. And, Candida, do you mean to be married in white satin or in a travelling-dress? I think white satin is the most economical in the long run, because it comes in as an evening dress afterwards."

"Oh, I don't know; I hadn't thought about it," said Candida, rather taken aback by this sudden change of topic. "You'll be very good to Ted, won't you, Sabina, because he really does deserve it? You won't let all the kindness be on his side?"

"Oh, you needn't be afraid. I shall spoil him horribly. I think ivory satin or bengaline would be best, don't you? And one could have a square-cut bodice, filled in with lace for the ceremony."

* * * * * *

The double wedding took place very quietly shortly after Christmas, the only guests being near relations of the contracting parties. Mr. and Mrs. Sylvester drove straight from the church door to Victoria, *en route* for Paris, where they were to spend a short honeymoon.

Paris! For the rest of her life that name called up in Candida's mind a confused vision of glittering theatres, glittering shops, glittering *cafés*, glaring sunshine and piercing winds, strange faces, strange voices, and strange manners. Nothing could have been better adapted than the novelty of her surroundings to draw her more closely to her husband, and make her feel her dependence upon him. It was not until long afterwards, when she could look back calmly upon that soul-shaking time, that she was able to realize how admirably Adrian had behaved. Some feminine streak in his own character helped him to adapt himself to the temperament of the woman he loved, while his naturally quick perception enabled him to decipher her moods, and to avoid jarring upon her susceptibilities. Altogether, it is doubtful whether, if he had been a man of more solid and substantial qualities, he would have acquitted himself so successfully in his new *rôle*.

After a fortnight spent in love-making and pleasure-seeking, both husband and wife felt as though they had suddenly awoke from some fantastic dream to prosaic reality when they found themselves in England once more, journeying down to the little suburban home, and the commonplace every-day existence that must perforce await them there. Although Candida wondered, with a touch of dull misgiving, how romance and sentiment were likely to fare under these unpromising conditions, she yet felt a certain sense of relief at the thought of entering upon a permanent and settled mode of existence by her husband's side, after the disturbed months of their engagement and the hurry and excitement of the Paris holiday. Though she hoped that Adrian would never be less her lover, she yet looked forward to the time when he would be more her friend—when, in short, they would no longer be irresponsible playfellows, dallying with life like children in a flower garden, but companions and helpmates, living in a work-a-day world, where duties and responsibilities occupied a larger place than pleasures or amusements.

Some such thoughts passed through her mind as they travelled down to Herne Vale together, mingled with an irrepressible desire that they were going to a home of their own, however modest; a couple of rooms in a dingy lodging-house would have more than contented her, if only she could have felt that they were her own. It would have been such happiness to keep house for Adrian, to make the rooms neat and pretty, to feel that she was working for him while he was working for her. She did not like to confess her longing to her husband, fearing that she would seem ungracious towards his mother; but, by some lover's instinct he answered, as he often did, her unspoken thoughts.

"Don't you wish we were still to be alone together?" he asked, as he leant his head upon her shoulder. "Yes, I can see you do, though you don't like to say so. Well, we'll have a home of our own some day—next year, perhaps, if things turn out as I hope. I shall work like a nigger now that I have got my most gracious sovereign lady to look after me, and keep me in order."

"I'm sure we shall be very happy with your mother," said Candida. "And I'm glad to think that our being there will be a help to her."

"Yes, she is charmed at having us, and the girls too; they are always called the girls, you know, though Louisa is forty, and Fanny a couple of years older. I only hope you won't find it intolerably dull. We shall always have the evenings together, of course, and on Saturdays we can go to the theatre, or take a run into the country."

"Oh, I shall be able to make myself happy whereever I am, as long as—as long as you don't get tired of me. I never feel as if I were the sort of woman to keep the love of a man like you. I am always the same; I can't pretend to be what I don't feel, and men are supposed to like variety."

"It is just the being always the same that makes your greatest charm," he said. "It is so restful to have to do with a woman whom one can depend upon, who is not a mere bundle of whims and moods. Caprices and vagaries are much more tiring in the long run than sameness—your kind of sameness, be it understood."

His tone was that of a man who has enjoyed a wide and varied experience, but Candida was not inclined to retrospective jealousy, so she laughed and allowed her misgivings to be coaxed away.

Candida had been down to Forest Lodge, her mother-in-law's house, several times in the course of her engagement, yet it was with something of a shock that she looked around her upon entering what was now to be her home. Forest Lodge was a small semi-detached villa, with a slip of a garden in front, in which grew one grimy sycamore. On one side of the narrow passage that was dignified by the name of hall, was a small square drawing-room, on the other side a small square dining-room. Gas was flaring in both rooms, on the night of the traveller's return, and the fresh odours of the coming supper mingled with the stale odours of the departed dinner.

Candida did her best to banish from her mind the critical thoughts which seemed like rank ingratitude in face of the warm welcome that greeted her. Mrs. Sylvester had scarcely eyes or ears except for her idolized son; but her daughters, Fanny and Louisa, hovered round their new sister-in-law, offering her everything they could think of, apologizing for all shortcomings, anxious to make themselves of use to her, yet fearful lest they should seem to be putting themselves forward. Their nervousness took the not uncommon form of excessive laughter, which Candida found rather disconcerting, since she had no intention of being amusing; still, she recognized that they meant to be very kind and conciliatory, and in the midst of her fatigue and embarrassment, was touched and comforted by the friendliness of her reception. She began to wonder what sort of characters the two plain, giggling, middle-aged women really possessed, and how they occupied their time. She had had but little experience of women of their age and circumstances, and inwardly resolved to try and enter into their interests, and share, if possible, their pursuits, since she, like them, would have no profession and no housekeeping to take up her time.

During the first two or three weeks at Forest Lodge, Candida felt herself too much in the position of a guest to be able to arrange her own life, or make any definite plans for the future. She was introduced to several of the Sylvesters' friends, and two or three little tea-parties were got up expressly to do her honour. Each Saturday she spent in town, passing the morning at the Gymnasium, and going to some place of amusement with her husband in the afternoon. Adrian was still as lover-like as in the early days of their engagement, and though he had settled down to work very steadily, yet as soon as office hours were over his only desire seemed to be to rush home to her side. His mother and sisters were never tired of telling Candida how beneficial her influence over him had proved. The dear boy had been a different creature since he had known her, they declared; it only showed that all he had needed to steady him and keep him out of mischief was a nice wife.

All this was gratifying enough, yet Candida could not help feeling some faint disappointment that she had been unable to persuade Adrian to take her into his confidence, and talk to her about his business affairs. She had made more than one attempt to lead the conversation round to financial topics when she sat with him in the smoking-room after dinner, but hitherto her efforts had all been baffled by the lover-like nonsense which formed the staple of his conversation almost as much now as in the days of their honeymoon.

One evening, about three weeks after their return, she went straight to the point that she had hitherto approached in roundabout fashion, and begged him to tell her about his work, and explain to her some of the mysteries of the Stock Exchange.

"I want to know about bulls and bears, and booms and slumps," she said. "Can't you explain to me the sort of things you do? I should like to understand how companies are started, and what the cover system really is."

"Oh, for heaven's sake, don't let us talk about such horrors now," he cried, with not unnatural shrinking from the proposed topic. "If you are really interested in such matters you can read the "Stock Exchange

Year Book," and the financial papers, and our monthly investment circular. Learn as much as you like about the beastly things, only don't expect me to talk shop in the bosom of my family."

Candida looked pained.

"I don't want to bother you," she said. "But I feel as if I had no part whatever in your real life, no share in your serious interests. Am I never to be anything but a sort of legalized mistress for you to kiss and coax when you have nothing more important to occupy you? Are we never to exchange a rational idea, or discuss anything but the shape of my nose and the colour of my eyes?"

He laughed good-humouredly.

"I'm sure we couldn't have more charming topics," he replied. "Darling, you look so nice when you are getting a little cross. I believe you know that a slight frown is extremely becoming to you. Your eyebrows look like two brown feathers that have blown together."

"Ah, you think you can silence me with flattery," she returned, shaking her head reproachfully at him.

"Do you know I have just discovered a new dimple beneath the corner of your left eye?" he observed irrelevantly. "It only appears when you smile in a particular way. Now, if there is one thing in woman I admire more than another, it is dimples. A really well-situated dimple covers a multitude of sins."

"I'm afraid I am getting fat," sighed Candida.

"That comes of leading such an idle life. I really must try and find some occupation; but none of the women about here seem to have anything to do, unless they are mothers of families."

"So much the better for them," said Adrian, lightly. "I wish I had nothing to do. Never mind, my dearest dear," he added quickly, as he perceived her perturbed expression; "we'll have a house of our own next year, and then you shall clean the windows and scrub the floors all day long, if you really wish it. Now, will you please smile again, because I want to kiss that new dimple?"

After this conversation Candida made a conscientious attempt to glean some knowledge of stocks and shares from the columns of the financial press, but the information thus gained was not exactly of an engaging nature; indeed, there came a time when she thought it wisest to discontinue her studies, and remain voluntarily in the dark. She next turned her attention to the only resource for the feminine unemployed—work among the poor. But it presently appeared that Mrs. Sylvester was afflicted with a nervous dread of dirt and infection, insomuch that her own daughters were only allowed to enter such of the houses of their poorer neighbours as were guaranteed to be clean and respectable by the clergyman of the parish. The district was not a poor one, and there was so large an army of voluntary workers that Candida recognized that her own efforts were quite superfluous. She gradually withdrew from the work when she found herself almost treading on the heels of other district-visitors in the best parlours of respectable women, who clearly needed nothing at her hands, and who scarcely took the trouble to conceal their contempt for the parochial doles.

For the space of a few weeks she shared, as far as possible, the occupations and amusements of her sisters-in-law. The life was so totally unlike anything to which she had hitherto been accustomed that at first its very novelty saved her from ennui. She felt as though she were plunged into the middle of some novel dealing with suburban life and society, and only needed to close the book when she wearied of the tedium and pettiness of the details therein described. Indeed, there was so strange an air of unreality about this new existence, owing, probably, to the lack of all regular employment, that she could hardly believe she would not awake some morning to find herself back in her Bloomsbury lodging, with a hard day's work before her.

But as the novelty wore off, the reality of her lot became more and more apparent, while she found it less easy to shut her eyes to its wearisome trivialities. Her curiosity as to the characters and pursuits of her new relations was soon satisfied, and with familiarity her amused interest changed to compassion and regret. Much as she appreciated the kindness and amiability of her sisters-in-law, it was only too clear to her that she could look for no real companionship from them. The two "girls" were accustomed to say that they had no time for reading, which meant that they had no inclination, wherefore it was not surprising that they were still mentally at the same level as when they left school at seventeen, having neither grown nor matured. Like too many of their kind, they were nothing more than good-humoured middle-aged school-girls, who still giggled over the tiny jokes, secrets, and mysteries that had delighted them a quarter of a century before.

Apart from bazaars, tea-parties, and church decorations, religion and ill-health formed the principal excitements of their lives. They fasted on Fridays, went regularly to early services, and were nearly always ailing; indeed, they seemed to regard chronic ill-health as the natural prerogative of women. Their doctor's and chemist's bills rivalled those of the butcher and grocer, while the trying of a new "treatment," or even of a quack remedy, was a source of never-failing delight. Until she perceived how much real enjoyment they derived from their ailments, Candida was quite concerned at the regularity with which colds, headaches, and bilious attacks succeeded each other in the family circle. The three ladies were seldom all free from sickness at the same time, and this fact seemed to constitute their only claim to interest and importance in their own eyes, and in those of their neighbours. Candida attributed their ill-health to their lack of occupation, and made up her mind that if, instead of existing with difficulty on a widow's and spinsters' pittance, they had only started a dancing-school or a Berlin-wool shop, they would now be enjoying the robust health and excellent spirits which distinguished the majority of the wage-earning women of her acquaintance. She soon became aware, however, that her new relations regarded the necessity for work as a downright degradation, and infinitely preferred leading the narrowest of existences on the narrowest of means, to earning a penny by their own exertions.

CHAPTER XV.

THE return of Mr. and Mrs. Ferrars from a lengthened wedding tour was quite an important event in the empty and purposeless existence to which Candida now found herself condemned. On her first visit to the little house in Hampstead in which the young couple had settled themselves, she found the bride in a great state of excitement over her new home, her new servants, and her new furniture. She could scarcely be induced to mention her husband, who had no longer any pretensions to the novelty of the rest of the establishment.

"Oh, Ted," she said at length, in reply to her friend's repeated inquiries—"Ted is all right, dear old thing! That reminds me, I must show you the lace he bought me at Venice. Yes, yes, of course, he is the best of husbands, positively without a flaw now that he has given up trying to talk to me as if I were an intellectual woman. At first he rather bored me by trying to get me to take an intelligent interest in the churches and pictures in Italy, but he soon saw that the task was hopeless, and took me to theatres instead. We used to look in at the shop windows all the morning, and in the afternoon he did the guide-book sights by himself while I rested. How sensible you were to spend all your time in Paris, where one need never be bothered with ruins or churches! I bought this frock in Paris. What do you think of it?"

"Very pretty," answered Candida, absently. "I suppose Ted is working very hard?"

"Oh, dreadfully. I never see anything of him except in the evenings, and then he yawns so, particularly if he takes me out anywhere, that I'm always afraid he will crack his jaws. I really must try and find some one else to take me about, and then he can yawn at home in peace."

"But would not that be rather dull for him, after working hard all day?"

"Oh, he really likes being dull, and he always has a lot of stupid old books that he wants to read. He tried to persuade me to begin what he calls a systematic course of reading, in order to improve my mind. He is so funny sometimes. Fancy me improving my mind!"

Candida looked a little uneasy.

"I hope you are very good to Ted," she said; "especially as he has turned out such a paragon of a husband. You are very happy together, aren't you?"

"Yes, of course. We get on like two turtle-doves, and he is perfectly devoted to me. But do just look at this cabinet, Candida. I got it in Wardour Street the other day; it's Chippendale or Sheraton, or something of the kind. Ted was rather horrified at the price, but it was really ridiculously cheap. Don't you think I'm a lucky girl, Candida? I wish you had a house of your own and nice things, instead of having to live with your husband's relations in a pokey place like Herne Vale."

"Yes, I must say I should like a house of my own," said Candida, rather wistfully. "Still, I am very happy, and all the more so for knowing that you are too."

Any slight uneasiness that she might have felt about the condition of the new *menage* was dispelled by the sight of Ted, who came home just in time to walk with her to the station. There could be no doubt that he was genuinely in love with his wife, and very proud of her beauty, which, he declared, had made quite a sensation at every hotel they stayed in during their tour. He evidently regarded her love of finery and amusement with an indulgent eye, considering that such little weaknesses were perfectly natural, and even becoming in so young and pretty a woman. He could afford to gratify her every reasonable wish, he explained, as long as he stuck closely to work, and that would not hurt him; indeed, he really enjoyed it.

It was about this time that Candida made up her mind to emancipate herself from the vortex of afternoon calls, tea-parties, and shopping excursions, in which she had been struggling since her arrival at Forest Lodge, and map out some more dignified form of existence for herself. A subscription to the London Library placed books once more within her reach, and she exchanged the little pottering walks, which her sisters-in-law regarded as constitutionals, for long lonely rambles, which carried her beyond the regions of villa-dom, out of sight even of the crystal monstrosity which dominated the landscape for miles around Herne Vale. With these resources she was able to pass her time not unpleasantly, the monotony of her existence being compensated for by the delightful "week-ends" which she and Adrian always spent together, and an occasional run up to town between whiles to visit some of her old friends, or take a class at the Gymnasium.

In spite of her revolt against the claims of Herne Vale society, and her lack of appreciation of suburban gaieties, Candida had contrived to win the confidence and affection of her mother and sisters-in-law. Her success, it is true, was partly due to a suppression of her own ideas and opinions—a piece of moral insincerity of which she was often ashamed. But discussion of any subject was impossible in that household if peace were to be maintained. She was compelled to treat the ladies much as if they were elderly children, humouring all their prejudices, and carefully avoiding any expression of opinion that would be likely to wound their very sensitive susceptibilities. They had, she discovered, their own well-defined views upon every abstract question that had come within their ken, and from these there could be no appeal, even though the views were never based upon reason or logic, but only upon the authority of some favourite clergyman, whose arguments were regarded as no less infallible than his office.

Candida's restraint of her naturally outspoken tongue was due, however, less to fear of giving offence than to a desire to avoid giving pain—a desire which was deepened and strengthened by a little confidence which accident caused her sisters-in-law to repose in her. Happening to meet them one day in a stationer's shop in Sydenham, she was surprised to see handed over the counter to them a large bundle of letters, which had evidently been addressed to the care of the proprietor. Their blushes, giggles, and guilty looks, as they followed her out of the shop, naturally roused her curiosity.

"I believe you two have been up to some mischief," she said laughingly. "You had better make a clean breast of it to me."

"Oh no, we couldn't possibly," said Louisa, nervously. "You would laugh at us, wouldn't she, Fanny? And I dare say you would be horribly shocked."

"I wonder whether she would?" returned Fanny, doubtfully. "After all, it was only a joke. Would you promise not to tell any one else if we told you—not even Adrian?"

"Oh yes, I promise," she answered carelessly. "You had better confide in me now I have seen the letters, or I shall think it something very dreadful."

"Yes, we had better tell her now," said Fanny. "You explain, Louie."

"No, I daren't," cried Louisa, giggling more uncontrollably than ever. "You do it, Fanny."

"Well, I don't know whether I can make you understand why we did it," began the elder sister, hesitatingly. "You ought to know the sort of lives we have always led, how we never went to dances, or saw much of —of gentlemen, because mamma disapproved of worldly ways."

"And we were never pretty or very attractive, even when we were quite young," put in Louisa. "And we had very little money to spend on clothes, because Adrian's education was so expensive."

"I've no doubt you always looked very nice," said Candida, wondering whither this preamble was leading.

"Perhaps we were really better and safer without beauty," said Louisa, with a sigh, "though it must be very pleasant to be admired and—and loved. Nobody ever fell in love with us, that we know of, though there was a curate once who was rather attentive to Fanny."

"Oh, how can you say such things?" exclaimed her sister, with an hysterical laugh. "I'm sure that was all your fancy, Louie; I never troubled my head about him. The long and the short of it is, Candida, that we neither of us ever had a lover; so, though we've read a lot about love in story-books, we haven't had any experience of it in real life. We often used to wonder what was in love-letters, and what proposals were like, and what engaged couples talked about. I dare say you will think it all very silly."

"No, I think it was perfectly natural," answered Candida, gently. "I used to wonder just the same before—before I knew."

"No! did you really?" said Fanny, visibly encouraged by this sympathetic reception of her confidences. "Well, we never thought we should be able to gratify our curiosity until a few months ago, when we happened to see a copy of a matrimonial newspaper. The advertisements amused us so much that I suggested—only in fun, you know—that we should each send an advertisement to the paper, just to see what sort of replies we should get. Of course, we never thought of answering any of them."

"But you don't mean to say that you really did it?" said Candida, uncertain whether to feel amused or scandalized.

"Yes, we really did. Louie described herself as a brunette of thirty, not pretty, but pleasant and domesticated, and with five hundred a year; and I said I was nineteen, tall and fair, with a Grecian nose and violet eyes."

"I had thirty-seven answers to mine, and Fanny only two," observed Louisa, not without complacency.

"Ah, but yours only wanted the money," put in the elder sister. "Mine were like real love-letters. They both wanted to have my photograph, and one of them asked me to meet him under the clock at Charing Cross."

"Well, I expect I've had more offers than any woman in Herne Vale," said Louisa. "There are not so many this time, I see. I put my fortune at two thousand a year, and they must have thought it was a hoax. Only five for me, and eleven for you, Fanny. Let me see, you were a widow of twenty-five, weren't you, with two hundred a year?"

Candida looked from one to the other, her heart filled with compassion for the two loveless little women, who had sought to brighten their stunted, colourless lives by means of counterfeit romances, and indignation against the customs that had rendered such a state of things possible. After all, she said to herself, these two women were not irredeemably plain, or rather, their lack of personal attraction was due not so much to any natural defects of face or figure as to the unhealthy conditions of their lives. Their features were passable, their figures straight and fairly proportioned. Vacuity of expression, dull eyes and hair, a sallow skin, a want of development, a mistaken taste in dress — it was to these defects that they owed their hopelessly uninteresting appearance. Had they received a vigorous education in their youth, and afterwards been given some object in life, some definite work to do in the world, instead of being condemned to lead the narrowest of semi-conventual existences, she could see no reason why they should not have turned out healthy, intelligent, pleasant-looking human beings, if nothing more. In the world of workers they would have found their own level, and made friends among the men and women with whom they were brought in contact. As things were, she could not bring herself to blame them for the peculiar method they had chosen of introducing a little romance into their grey lives; yet she felt that it would be as well to prevent a repetition of the doubtful experiment.

"Now that you have gratified your curiosity," she remarked, "I suppose you won't care to go on with these advertisements? There is a certain amount of risk connected with the joke, because one of your would-be suitors might wait outside the shop to see who came to fetch the letters, and follow you home."

"Oh, what a dreadful idea!" cried the sisters both at once, glancing nervously over their shoulders. "Do you think any one was there to-day? No, we shan't care to do it again."

"There's the tram," said Louisa. "I think we had better take it, or Fanny will be over-tired. Dr. Matthews called just before we left home, and he said she was suffering from nervous debility. He has ordered her a course of iron and quinine."

"I am sorry to hear it," said Candida, longing to suggest that more air and exercise, and the healthier appetite consequent thereupon, would probably benefit the invalid more than tons of tonics.

She was beginning to be quite ashamed of her own appetite, for the three ladies ate like sparrows, and, with the exception of dinner, the meals provided were of the scantiest description. It was evident that Mrs. Sylvester's means were very narrow, and Candida felt glad to think that the payments made by Adrian must be some help to her; besides, his presence in the house ensured the appearance of one sufficient meal every day. She herself was often obliged to supplement the breakfasts and luncheons out of her own pocket, and for this and other purposes found the advantage of her father's allowance, since Adrian never seemed to have any ready money to spare. He had told her soon after their return to put down any purchases that she might make to his account. But as she had a morbid horror of debt, this arrangement had the effect of keeping her expenditure strictly within the limits of her allowance.

It was upon the subject of finance that she and her husband had their first little disagreement. Adrian came home one evening overflowing with enthusiasm about the prospects of a commercial company which was shortly to be floated by some friends of his. The Automatic Cork-drawing Company, Limited, was expected to make the fortunes of every one connected with it, and Adrian only regretted that he had but a small sum at his disposal to invest in so promising a speculation.

After dinner, when he and Candida were alone together, he continued to descant upon the advantages held out by the new undertaking.

"I should like to give my friends a chance of sharing in the luck," he observed at length. "Do you think your father would care to invest a few hundreds?"

"No, I'm sure he wouldn't, even if he had them," she replied with decision. "He hates speculations, and he never has any money to spare."

"But he might easily raise some—say a thousand, or even five hundred. He would probably double his capital in three months, and then he could clear out. There would be practically no risk, as long as he knew when to run."

"Then do you mean that there would be risk for the people who bought the shares of him?"

"Oh, that would depend on how long they held on; of course, they would have to look out for themselves. You might write and tell your father about it. It would be an advantage to me as well as to him, because the directors have promised to put business in my way if I bring them a certain amount of capital."

"It would be quite useless," she answered. "He hasn't got the money, and if he had he wouldn't put it into a company that was to be boomed for a few weeks, only to smash up as soon as the promoters had cleared out."

"You don't understand anything about business," he said, with gentle reproach. "And you really might trust my judgment in these matters. Of course, I don't want your father to do anything shady; I was merely proposing a perfectly legitimate speculation for our mutual benefit. You have often said you wished you could be of use to me; now here is your chance."

"There is nothing that would give me more happiness than to be able to help you," she said; "but you are mistaken in thinking that this is my chance. If you knew my father as well as I do, you would understand that to make him such a proposal would be simply a waste of ink and paper."

"That's the worst of these country gentlemen," grumbled Adrian. "They never have any notion of business. Consols at two and three-quarters are their idea of a lucrative investment. And then they are surprised to find themselves hard up."

"City men are not always in flourishing circumstances," returned Candida. "There is such a thing as being too clever."

"There's something in that," he said, with a good-humoured laugh. "Well, I'm sorry you don't see your way to helping me in this little matter. However, I dare say I shall be able to raise the money elsewhere."

CHAPTER XVI.

WITH the approach of summer the question of a holiday, which yearly agitates the breast of every Londoner, became the subject of discussion at Forest Lodge. Mrs. Sylvester at once announced her intention of remaining quietly at home; it was a trouble to move, she explained, and the Herne Vale air was so fine that there was really no necessity for a change. Adrian having no money to spend on travelling expenses, it was decided that the young couple should take advantage of a standing invitation to Branksmead, and Candida laid a secret plan of inducing her mother to ask Fanny and Louisa to spend a fortnight there by turns. It was finally arranged that she should go home first alone, and that Adrian should follow her in about a week's time.

Mr. St. John greeted his daughter upon her arrival with an air of tender sympathy, almost of commiseration, which made her laugh; it seemed so comically inappropriate.

"You are looking much better than I expected,"

he said, as they wandered round the garden after dinner. "You are really happy—still? Your illusions are not shattered—yet? I never thought that your spirits would survive six months of a suburban home, a mother-in-law, and a stock-broking husband."

"Why not?" asked Candida. "My mother-in-law is the kindest little woman in the world, and we have not had a single jar. As for Adrian, he is the most devoted of husbands, and it is not his fault that he was brought up to a business career. He is working very steadily now, and he spends every minute of his spare time with me. He hasn't tired of me yet," she added, with a little nod of triumph. "He still thinks me the most beautiful and fascinating of my sex."

"Well, well," sighed her father, "I only hope the idyll will last."

"I believe you are quite disappointed because Adrian has not begun to beat me yet," laughed Candida. "But you must remember that I am nearly as big as he is, and in much better training. I think thé idyll will last," she added, lowering her voice, "because —because I hope that a great happiness is coming to us. I have just told mother, but no one else knows, not even Adrian. I thought I should like to tell him down here."

"Oh, you poor dear child!" said her father, putting his arm round her. "What risks women do run when they marry. Dear, dear, I wish Branksmead were not entailed upon the Foley St. Johns. I should have liked your boy to have it."

"Oh, he will be better off fighting his own way in the world with a free hand than trying to prop up a falling house," said Candida. "He shall have a good education if I can manage it, and if he has good health, he will need no other heritage. I have begun to make plans already," she added with a smile.

"But what if it is a girl?"

"Oh, the same plans will serve. If I had half a dozen children, I shouldn't make any difference between the education and opportunities given to the sons and the daughters. I would never see the girls sacrificed to the boys, only to be rewarded with brotherly ingratitude and contempt."

As soon as Adrian arrived, Candida hastened to confide her secret to him. Watching for his eyes to brighten with joy and pride at her intelligence, she could hardly believe her own senses when she saw his countenance fall, and heard him mutter—

"Good heavens! this is a deuced awkward complication."

"You—you are not glad," she faltered. "But surely you must have realized that this was a very probable event."

"Well, upon my soul, I'd scarcely given it a thought," he answered gloomily. "Anyhow, I never imagined it would be so soon. Other good-looking young married women don't have these misfortunes. It will quite spoil your beauty, and age you by years. And then the expense! It will nearly double our rate of living, and that little house will be quite uninhabitable."

"Of course, we must have a home of our own now; at least, we ought to get into one before Christmas. I shall be sorry to leave your mother, and we must try and help her as much as we can, but she will quite understand that we cannot possibly stop on there."

"Oh, but we must; it would be impossible to move at present," he said decidedly. "I simply haven't got the money. We shall have to make shift as best we can. I must give up my dressing-room, I suppose, and the girls will have to sleep together. I must say it's confoundedly awkward just now; I shouldn't have minded so much half a dozen years hence."

"I'm sorry it causes you such intense annoyance," she said coldly. "But it is rather strange that you shouldn't have thought of this contingency before you married."

Fearing lest her powers of self-control should give way, she turned and left him. With all her desire to see her husband in the best light, and to make allowance for his shortcomings, she could not help feeling bitterly hurt at the manner in which he had received her news. He had not appeared to realize that the child was his as much as hers, but seemed to regard its advent as an error of taste for which she alone was responsible. All her natural pleasure in the prospect of motherhood was temporarily dimmed by this unexpected lack of sympathy in the one human being from whom, above all others, she had a right to expect it.

Candida had by no means recovered her spirits when she met her husband again at the dinner-table, but Adrian, who was keenly sensitive to any coolness in the social atmosphere, took an early opportunity of making his peace with her.

The news had taken him by surprise, he explained, and he was anxious about her safety, as well as worried over money affairs. But he admitted that it was very absurd to be taken aback by such a natural occurrence, and no doubt the luck would turn before long. Anyhow, she was to forget what he had said, and not to treat him as if he were a long way off, or suffering from an infectious disease, because that kind of thing made him very uncomfortable. And Candida allowed herself to be soothed and pacified, being quite incapable of perceiving that his desire for a reconciliation lay not so much in a real feeling of tenderness as in his dislike of any unpleasantness in his social surroundings.

The arrival of Louisa upon a fortnight's visit took off her thoughts from herself and her own troubles, for her sister-in-law was as *gauche* with strangers as a girl of sixteen, and all Candida's energies were bent on making her feel happy and at home. Adrian, who entertained a wholesome fear of his father-in-law, and found the Hall decidedly dull, spent a good deal of his time at the Vicarage, where Sabina had been staying for the past fortnight, while Ted ran down for the Sundays.

"I never realized till quite lately what good company your husband was," remarked Mrs. Ferrars one day to her friend. "Of course, last summer he was entirely engrossed by you, so that I had no opportunity of discovering his talents. He is such a contrast to Ted, who is virtue personified, but a trifle solid. He never seems to want any amusement, but would be contented to spend all the evenings for the rest of his life by the domestic hearth. Oh, those domestic evenings! I begin to think it is a pity I gave up the stage when I married; I had forgotten how interminable evenings at home really could seem."

"Ted would never have agreed to your continuing to act," said Candida. "For one thing, he would have seen nothing of you, as he has to be out all day. Besides, he is much too old-fashioned to tolerate the idea of his wife working for money as long as he can afford to maintain her."

"Then he ought not to mind paying my bills," grumbled Sabina.

"But does he?"

"Well, he never says much, but he looks surprised at the 'demned total.' He might see that as I've nothing else to do, I must go in for dress and society; I'm simply driven to it. And he ought not to think it a hardship to take me out in the evenings, or be left alone at home. He forgets how dull I've been all day, with nothing to do and no one to speak to."

"You will be all right when you have children," observed Candida. "Wifehood isn't a sufficient occupation for an able-bodied woman, but I believe motherhood is."

"Don't talk of anything so dreadful," cried Sabina. "I want to have a little more fun before I'm laid on the shelf for life. Oh, here comes your Adrian. You never told me what a splendid mimic he was. He can take off the vicar to the life, and most of the funny old people in the village."

Candida flushed uncomfortably. She did not enjoy the idea of her old friends being held up to ridicule.

The subject of her conversation with Sabina left an uneasy impression upon her mind, with the result that she took advantage of Ted's next visit to Branksmead to have a confidential talk with him. She found him, as she had expected, a little inclined to be plaintive on the subject of his wife and her requirements.

"I don't wish to say a word against Sabina," he began, using the time-honoured preamble to a marital complaint. "She is a dear, good girl, and we are as fond of each other as ever; but I do think that she is just the least bit exacting. If I work hard all day to keep her in comfort, it is rather unreasonable to expect me to take her out nearly every evening. I think she might be contented to bear me company in her own home. You might as well put a horse to plough in the daytime, and expect him to perform in a circus at night."

"I dare say it does seem rather hard," said Candida, thoughtfully. "But I suppose it is natural that she should crave for a little excitement, considering how stimulating her life has been during the past few years. And remember, that while you are working at an interesting profession, Sabina is engaged in a much more wearisome pursuit; I mean, in doing nothing."

"She has her house and servants to look after."

"Yes, but no human being can spend twelve or fourteen hours a day in ordering a dinner for two persons."

"I wish she had a taste for reading, like you," he said. "I don't believe she ever reads anything but novels and society papers. Yet she is naturally very quick and clever; she might be an excellent companion if only she would give herself a chance."

"Well, you see," returned Candida, apologetically, "girls are always having it dinned into them that men hate clever women, so, naturally, they try to appear as silly and ignorant as they possibly can. Man's taste, we know, is woman's test. If you happen to prefer a cultivated intelligent human being to a human goose, why, you must expect to suffer for the eccentricity of your taste. But as for Sabina, she is really clever enough for two; she only pretends to be silly because she likes to be popular."

"Yes," he said, his face softening, "of course she likes gaiety and fun better than books or serious talk. She is so young and pretty, it is only natural she should want to enjoy herself, and I don't really grudge it to her, though I do grumble now and then. She will grow old and sober down quite soon enough, and then we shall be able to play Darby and Joan for the rest of our lives."

CHAPTER XVII.

THE return to Herne Vale marked the beginning of a new epoch in Candida's life. Her long walks had to be curtailed, and part of the time hitherto bestowed upon her books was now devoted to a more domestic occupation. She was learning to sew, and proving herself a very dull pupil. Nothing but the most dogged industry and determination could have brought those strong unpractised fingers to set dainty stitches and run Liliputian tucks. But though progress was slow and painful, the art was gradually acquired, and Candida declared that since the day on which she had first succeeded in circling round the three trapezes, she had never felt so proud and triumphant as when she made a tiny frock alone and unaided, and was assured by her mother-in-law that it was "not at all bad."

It was well that she had so engrossing an occupation to divert her attention from the clouds that had begun to gather upon her horizon. It was a time of general depression, if not panic, in the financial world, and Adrian looked every day more anxious and harassed. He was often detained late at the office, and occasionally dined and slept in town. The Saturday outings had been given up, partly because ready money was so scarce, partly because they were not thought prudent in the present state of Candida's health. Adrian, though almost invariably courteous and considerate to his wife, had gradually relinquished his lover-like ways, and no longer showed any special desire for her society. Candida tried to shut her eyes to his growing indifference, and to console herself with the thought that the alteration in his behaviour was chiefly due to his preoccupation with business worries. She assured herself that when their affairs improved, and still more when their child was born, the old affection would revive, and all would be well with them once again.

A few weeks after their return, however, an incident occurred which sowed fresh seeds of uneasiness in her mind. Having occasion to go to town for a morning's shopping, she took the opportunity of paying a long-promised visit to her former colleague, Miss Mason, who had lately taken a flat at Earl's Court. That lady, declaring that her visitor must be moped to death at Herne Vale, and that a glimpse of the world would do her good, had insisted upon carrying her off to Olympia. There they were to have tea, and amuse themselves for an hour with the humours of the crowd. But the humours of the crowd turned out to be rather more sensational than Candida had either expected or desired.

At a little table, not far from that at which the two friends had settled themselves, a man and a girl were seated. The girl was pretty and quietly dressed, with a touch of refinement about her manner and appearance. The man was sitting with his back to Candida; but his figure was too familiar an aspect to leave her for an instant in doubt as to his identity. It was her husband.

A sensation of sickness and dizziness stole over her as she noticed the *empressement* of his manner towards his companion, and his evident delight in her society; it was so exactly the attitude that he had assumed towards herself when they visited such places together, only a few short months before.

The pair were obviously wrapped up in each other; and Candida's heart ached as she saw the girl's eyes melt and soften when she met her companion's glance. Presently a bunch of Neapolitan violets was transferred from Adrian's coat to the front of the girl's black dress. Violets! Candida started as she remembered that her husband had more than once breathed the name of Violet in his sleep. She had guessed that a Violet must have been among his early loves, but she had never cared to question him upon the subject.

"I—I am tired," she said to her friend. "I think I had better go home now. I can catch the five-thirty from Victoria."

On her arrival at Forest Lodge she found a telegram from Adrian to say that business would keep him at the office until late, and that he should dine and sleep in town. It was not until the next evening that she had the opportunity of a few words alone with him.

"You have never inquired how I got on in town yesterday," she began, speaking with a nervousness that was more on his account than her own. "After I finished my shopping, I went to see Miss Mason, and she insisted on taking me to tea at Olympia."

He started slightly, and threw a quick glance at her.

"Olympia!" he said, with assumed carelessness. "Wasn't that rather imprudent?"

"I don't think I'm the worse for it. I wanted to tell you that I saw you there. I suppose you didn't see me?"

"No; I saw no one I knew except the acquaintance I was with. Did you notice her?"

"Yes, I thought she was very pretty. I wondered if she was Violet."

"Violet!" he repeated, turning sharply upon her. "What do you know about Violet? Has any one been trying to make mischief between us?"

"No; you are the only person that has ever mentioned her to me. You have sometimes uttered her name in your sleep. I should not have said anything about it if I had not seen you yesterday with a girl to whom you gave some violets. Does she know that you are married?"

"Yes—no—I forget; but you really needn't trouble your head about her. She is a little girl whom I had a flirtation with long ago, before I knew you. I hadn't seen her for ages, till I met her in Oxford Street yesterday; and she asked me to take her to Olympia for old acquaintance' sake. As I told you, I was obliged to stop and dine with a fellow at the Club, so I thought I might as well spend the afternoon at Olympia as anywhere else. Perhaps I was foolish; but you don't think it so very wrong, do you, now that you know the whole story?"

"No, of course not," agreed Candida. "Yet—yet I can't help thinking about that poor girl; she had such a pretty, pathetic little face, and looked so overflowing with happiness at being with you. I think you ought to tell her you are married; it might save her from a great disappointment."

"What a queer girl you are!" he said, looking at her with mingled amusement and surprise. "Most women would have been ready to scratch her eyes out of her head. The fact of my marriage doesn't concern her in the slightest degree, and there's no occasion for you to worry about her at all. She's not a lady, you know, only a little girl out of a shop, and she probably goes out with a different fellow every Saturday afternoon."

Candida was silent for a moment. She was only too willing to believe her husband's statement, yet she could not forget what she had seen with her own eyes.

"I don't want you to think me foolishly suspicious," she said at length. "Only I couldn't help fancying that you were attracted by this girl, and I wanted to tell you that I could understand that—that you may have difficulties and temptations to contend with, which you would naturally shrink from confiding to me. I have often thought that to a man, and particularly a man of your temperament, the calm affection of married life must seem sober prose indeed compared with the glamour and romance of dawning love. Don't you remember the days when you and I were just hovering on the borders of passion, when everything was vague, tentative, uncertain, when our silence said so much more than our speech, and when the touch of our hands seemed to reveal hidden secrets in life? And don't you remember the first word of love, how it altered the aspect of the whole world? and the first kiss, what a soul-shaking event it was? Nothing can ever equal the early spring of love, and I can quite understand that a man, without being naturally sensual or inconstant, may feel an irresistible desire to repeat the experience."

She paused, but Adrian was staring into the fire, and did not speak.

"Even I," she went on hesitatingly—"yes, even I

a woman, and therefore by nature and training colder and more self-restrained than a man, have sometimes felt that if a lover, young, impetuous and adoring as you were in early days, were to set himself to win me from my allegiance, it might cost me a sharp struggle to resist him, to shut my heart to all the delights of unfamiliar tenderness, all the glories of a newly-awakened love."

"You dare to tell me that!" cried Adrian, the blood rushing to his face.

"Perhaps it is foolish to be so frank, even with one's husband. But I only wanted to show you that I could enter into what seem to be very natural feelings, and make allowance for involuntary weaknesses. If I knew that you were harassed and beset by any temptation that you were trying to resist, I should be so ready and willing to help you if I could. I would not look for any signs of affection at such a time, nor be hurt by any coldness or neglect. Only let me know the truth, and you will never find me hard or unforgiving. And if the warning does not come too late, stop before you lead that poor pretty thing into any trouble. It is easy to see that you have won her fancy, and I should not imagine that she had a very strong character, so that it is for you to protect her against herself."

"You talk as if she were your sister," he said, with rather a forced laugh. "But I tell you the girl is nothing to me, nor I to her, so far as I know. So pray make your mind easy on the subject."

"Of course, I believe you," she answered. "You pride yourself on being a man of honour, and therefore you would not stoop to lie to a woman, even though she is your wife."

He flushed slightly, and his eyes dropped before hers, but he only answered carelessly—

"That is a good, sensible girl. I knew you were not likely to make a fuss about nothing; I have always found you willing to listen to reason."

CHAPTER XVIII.

EARLY in the new year the time of trial came and passed, and was straightway forgotten in the joy and pride of motherhood. The child was a boy, as Candida had hoped, the world being, as she sometimes said, not yet ripe for women. The young mother had done marvellously well, according to the doctor who attended her, and who, being a conservative, old-fashioned man, felt but a grudging admiration for her splendid physique and elastic constitution. He was not at all sure that he approved of such comparative immunity from pain and weakness at the time of peril. In his opinion there was something unfeminine about it; the Churching service would lose all meaning if the majority of women were like Mrs. Sylvester, and the most lucrative branch of the medical profession would be shorn of much of its profit. Still, he could not deny that his patient was as happy and devoted a mother as any of the "womanly" women who so nearly slipped through his fingers, and wrung even his callous old heart in their hour of agony.

When Candida was about again the Branksmead party came up to spend the day, and make the acquaintance of the new member of the family. The boy, who was to be called Roland, after his grandfather, had received unlimited admiration and adulation of an undiscriminating nature from the female members of his household, but his father had hitherto held aloof, criticized the shape of his nose and the size of his mouth, and positively refused to handle him. But Mr. St. John, much to the young mother's delight, took his grandson fearlessly in his arms, examined his points, carefully measured him from top to toe, and ordered up the kitchen scales to weigh him in. When he was solemnly pronounced to be three pounds heavier, and an inch and a half longer than the normal male infant of his age, Candida became as radiant as a young *débutante* who hears that she has been adjudged the belle of her first ball.

"He will be just like you, father," she said—"a true St. John. Look what broad shoulders, and what a deep chest he has. And his spine is so strong that he tries to sit up already."

It was a material addition to Candida's happiness that she was at ease for the moment about the extra expenses entailed upon the household. Her godmother had sent her a cheque which covered the doctor's and nurses' fees, and enabled her to lay by a portion of her allowance to meet future calls upon her purse. There was a nursemaid to be hired, a baby-carriage to be bought, and then it was so hard to pass unheeding those tempting shop-windows in which were displayed the most fairy-like of embroideries, the daintiest of cloaks and hoods. Though she sometimes fell a victim to vicarious vanity, she restrained her extravagant impulses to the best of her ability, for there were many necessary demands upon her small means. Apparently the depression still continued in the money-market, for Adrian made no proposal to contribute anything towards her personal expenses.

"I can manage to pay the nurse's wages out of my allowance as long as you are short of money," she had told him, when that functionary was first engaged. "But, of course, you will arrange with your mother about payment for the extra expense that we shall cause her. There is the nurse's board, you know, and more should be paid for my keep for some months to come."

"I will see to it; you needn't trouble about it," Adrian had replied. "In fact, I have already settled the matter with my mother. You had better not speak to her on the subject, as it only makes her uncomfortable. By the way," he added after a pause, "you must be rather dull now that you are tied at home so much. Wouldn't you like to invite a friend down here for a few days? I dare say Mrs. Ferrars would come if you asked her; Ted must be on circuit just now."

Candida fell in with the suggestion readily enough, feeling touched and grateful by her husband's thoughtfulness on her account. Sabina accepted the invitation, and brought her pretty face, her smart frocks, and her high spirits to enliven the little household for the space of a week. She was looking particularly well, and seemed more contented than she had been in the summer. Ted, she explained, was very much improved; in fact, he was turning into quite a model husband.

"He lets me go out as much as I like," she said; "pays my bills without a murmur, and never tries to make me read improving books. He seems to have made up his mind to take me as I am, and make the best of me."

"I hope he gets rewarded for his good behaviour," observed Candida.

"Oh yes, I always give him good dinners, and see that his buttons are sewn on. He ought to be satisfied, because men always give out that all they want in a wife is a pretty good-tempered woman who will attend to their creature comforts."

"Yes, but Ted is different from the average man," said Candida, thoughtfully. "He used to have ideas about making a companion of his wife; he never gave out that he wanted a useful toy or an ornamental housekeeper."

"Well, that's very much what he has got," laughed Sabina. "But, of course, the supply corresponds with the demand, and the individual must expect to suffer if his demands are above those of his fellows."

Adrian, who, in his character of host, had exerted himself to entertain the visitor, and make her stay agreeable to her, relapsed after her departure into more unsociable ways. He seemed to take but the faintest interest in his child, and spent the greater part of his time in town. His health began to deteriorate again, and Candida realized with bitter disappointment that she no longer had the slightest influence over him, and that the birth of their child had not had the expected result of binding them more closely together. Still, she had no overt wrong to complain of. Her husband, when at home, was invariably pleasant and courteous both to herself and to his mother and sisters, but at the same time he availed himself of every opportunity of escaping from the domestic circle, and Candida could hardly bring herself to blame him for his neglect. Now that love had died out between them, the society of three women and a baby must, she realized, prove insupportably dull to a man of his age and temperament.

This vaguely unsatisfactory period lasted for some weeks, and then a new experience befell her. Adrian had gone to dine at a bachelor-party given by a stockbroker friend in the neighbourhood, and had left orders that no one should sit up for him. About two o'clock Candida, sleeping with her child in the room that was now called the night-nursery, was awakened by the sound of voices in the front garden, and the turning of the key in the lock.

"There, now you're all right, aren't you, old fellow?" said a strange voice. "Good night. Hope you won't be the worse for this to-morrow."

The door creaked on its hinges, and there was the sound of uncertain steps in the hall below. Candida listened for the scratch of a lucifer, but hearing nothing but the noise of collisions with the hall furniture, got up, fearing she scarcely knew what, and went downstairs. She found her husband apparently searching for the matchbox in the umbrella-stand.

"That you, my dear?" he said with a curiously pompous inflection on perceiving her. "Sorry to have dish-disturbed you so late. Great deal of business talk after dinner—great deal—great——"

He gave a slight lurch towards her, but instantly recovered himself, and stood more rigidly upright than before.

"Couldn't find the mash-matchbox," he went on, still with the same portentous solemnity of tone. "It's such a—such a silly mashbox."

He gave a sudden unexpected little titter, which Candida, much to her own surprise, involuntarily echoed. Her husband's condition was now only too obvious, and her first sensation was one of relief that the sight of him no more aroused in her a feeling of scorn or disgust than would the sight of a delirious fever patient, or an encounter with an "innocent" in a village street. Had she still loved him the spectacle of him as he now was might have gone near to breaking her heart; but as things were, only her feminine instincts of compassion and helpfulness were called forth by the sight of his infirmity, and the efforts of the human in him to assert itself over the fuddled brute, or, at least, to conceal the fuddlement. Her only thought was how she could best aid him in that pathetic struggle, support his tottering self-respect, and keep up the illusion that there was nothing unusual in his manner or appearance.

"Yes, some matchboxes are silly," she agreed, scarcely knowing what she said, so anxious was she to "play up to him" in the squalid little drama. "I will light your candle. You must be quite tired out after so much business talk, and longing to get to bed."

She put her hand under his arm, and guided his uncertain steps to the foot of the staircase. With the support of the banisters on one side, and herself on the other, she thought that he would be capable of making the ascent without any such noise as would be likely to alarm the household. But, to her dismay, he halted at the bottom of the flight, and bent his knees as though he were about to sit down on the lowest step.

"Yes, very exhausting evening," he murmured indistinctly. "And most unsatis—satisfractry. Some of the other fellows—took too mush—mush too mush—to drink. Such a sad sight—painful sight."

"Yes, it must have been," agreed Candida, holding him on his feet by main force, for if once he sat down she was afraid she would be unable to get him on his legs again without assistance. "I am afraid you are feeling a little faint—I dare say the room was hot—but try and walk upstairs. You will be so much more comfortable in bed, and I want to get back to baby before he wakes."

Fortunately his natural instincts of courtesy and compliance, so far from being destroyed, were rather accentuated by his condition. The entreaty in his wife's voice had power to reach his brain through the fumes that obscured it. By a determined effort of his half-stupefied will, he planted his foot on the first stair, and, partly carried, partly dragged by his wife, struggled up to the top with less noise than might have been expected.

But even now Candida's troubles were not at an end. The sight of the half-open door of the night-nursery, and the light burning within, started a new train of thought in her husband's mind.

"I want to go and say goo—night to my little son," he remarked in sentimental tones. "Just to kish—kiss him in his sleep."

"No, no; you would wake him," said Candida,

hastily, shuddering at the very idea of that spirituous breath scorching her baby's cheek. "Wait till tomorrow morning."

"Oh, you *are* unkind," said Adrian, reproachfully, as she guided him into his own room, " not to let me k sh my little son."

He suddenly sat down on the end of the bed, and burst into tears. Candida, recognizing that it would be useless to reason with him, knelt down and pulled off his muddy boots, while he sat with his hands covering his face, and the tears streaming through his fingers. When at length she had contrived, with infinite toil and difficulty, to get him into bed, he sank almost at once into a heavy, uneasy slumber. Fearing to leave him alone, lest he should wake, and try to light a candle, or wander about the house, she opened the door into her own room, that she might hear if her child cried, and then established herself in an armchair, where she sat till dawn, listening to the stertorous breathing of the man on the bed.

The next morning Adrian did not make his appearance at the breakfast-table.

"He was late last night," explained Candida. "And he has a bad headache this morning. He will be down presently, but he doesn't feel equal to going up to town."

She threw a furtive glance at her mother-in-law, and encountered another as furtive.

"Adrian has always been subject to bad headaches," observed Mrs. Sylvester; "and late hours never did agree with him."

When at last Adrian made his appearance, Candida could with difficulty express a shiver of disgust as she noted his swollen bloodshot eyes and sodden skin. His shaking hand could hardly carry his cup to his mouth, and it was with difficulty that he choked down a few morsels of dry toast. His mother and sisters were full of pity for his evident sufferings, and Candida felt that they regarded her as hard and callous because she did not join the chorus of sympathy and regret.

When at length she was left alone with her husband, he looked up at her with a deprecatory smile.

"I'm afraid I gave you a lot of bother last night," he said. "I can only urge as an excuse for my conduct, that it's the first time I've come home like that since we were married, and that's fifteen months ago."

"You have been very considerate," she replied.

"You can't judge a man by a woman's standard, you know," he went on. "At least, if you tried to you'd make him less of a man than a molly-coddle."

She looked at him for a moment, but answered nothing. He was quick enough to understand her unspoken thought.

"You're thinking that I'm not a particularly brilliant specimen of manhood this morning," he said good-humouredly. "Well, I'm afraid I'm hardly in a fit state to argue the point. I feel all head and and no legs."

The amiability of his mood, taken in conjunction with his obvious physical discomfort, did not fail to make its impression on Candida's mind, in spite of her natural feeling of repulsion and distaste. Her sense of justice, no less than of generosity, urged her to give credit where credit was due; besides, the fact that a man was down was, in her opinion, a reason for giving him a fillip rather than a kick.

"You are the best-tempered person I ever met, man or woman," she observed. "I hope our boy will inherit a share of your amiability."

Adrian stared at her for a moment, scarcely able to believe his ears, her character being as completely a riddle to him as in the first hour of their acquaintance. He had expected, been fully prepared for blame and reproaches, but to hear instead of either an aspiration that her idolized child might be like him in any particular, constituted a treatment that puzzled and well-nigh alarmed him.

"The heir-apparent will be well-advised to take after his mother," he said lightly. "You're a good fellow, Candida; most women would have nagged my head off this morning. Ugh, that must have been vile champagne of Warner's; it couldn't have been the whisky. We had liqueurs, though, and they always play the deuce with me."

He looked so sick and sorry, that the ministering impulse awoke again in Candida's breast.

"You'd like some soda-water," she said. "I'll fetch you a bottle. And hadn't you better lie down, and have an eau-de-Cologne-and-water bandage on your head? Then if I read aloud to you for a little while you'll probably go to sleep. That's how I used to doctor Sabina when she had a headache."

"When she had been making a night of it, I thought you were going to say," he laughed, as he threw himself on the sofa. "Did our lovely Sabina ever make a night of it, I wonder? Dear Candida," he added, as she brought him the soda-water, "I'm so awfully obliged to you for giving me a cooling drink instead of a scolding. I can't think how you can resist the temptation to say a word in season, or something equally unpleasant, entirely for my own good."

"I used to think a woman might influence a man for his own good," she answered; "but that was when I was a foolish inexperienced girl. I am wiser now. If you can disregard the warnings your doctor has given you, you will heed no words of mine."

CHAPTER XIX.

EASTER fell late that year. The spring months had been unusually sultry, and the small rooms at Forest Lodge felt almost unbearably warm and close. Candida began to long for a breath of country air, both on her own account and upon that of her child, whose cheeks were gradually losing their colour and roundness. Branksmead was always open to her; but she shrank from going home now, knowing that she could no longer meet her father's eyes, and assert that she was still happy in her marriage. It was a great relief, therefore, when Adrian announced one day that a friend had offered to lend him a cottage in Surrey for the Easter holidays.

"It's an out-of-the-way place, I believe," he said, "and a long way from the station. But I'm told that there's a large garden, and the air is said to be good."

"Oh, it sounds delightful!" cried Candida. "It will be the very thing for Roley. I have been longing to take him away somewhere."

"It will be precious dull," observed Adrian,

"Couldn't we ask some lively person to come and cheer us up? We shall have a spare room."

"I thought you would ask one of your sisters, if there was room. Fanny would be the better for a change."

"Good heavens!" he exclaimed. "We don't want to take the whole family with us when we go out for a holiday. Besides, Fanny is going to stay with a friend at Sutton, and Louisa will be wanted at home. No; can't you suggest some one who would keep up our spirits and her own too? It had better be a woman, because a man would be bored by the baby."

Candida considered for a moment.

"Most of my friends are working women, who would only get a few days at Easter," she said. "I can't think of any one except Sabina; but I fancy Ted would be at home, and she might not like to leave him."

"Probably not," returned Adrian, carelessly. "But it might be just worth while asking her. If she can't come, we must try and find somebody else."

But, as it turned out, Sabina was able to accept the invitation. Ted, it appeared, had arranged to go for a walking tour with a couple of friends, so that she would be left alone. She should thoroughly enjoy having Candida and the dear baby all to herself. She supposed that Mr. Sylvester would have to go up to town nearly every day.

The holiday passed off pleasantly enough. The

cottage was comfortable, the neighbourhood abounded in woods and commons, while the weather was sufficiently accommodating to allow the visitors to spend most of their time out of doors. Candida contented herself for the most part with the garden and the nearest lanes, where she could wheel Roley in his carriage, while the others took long rambles and explored the surrounding country. The only drawback to the outing was the fact that Sabina was obliged to cut short her visit at the end of ten days, and return to town. The servants had been quarrelling, she explained, in response to entreaties that she would stay till the end of the fortnight; and there was something wrong with the kitchen boiler. She must get home before Ted, and see that the household machinery was in working trim.

The blank left by the removal of her lively presence was so keenly felt by the friends she had deserted that both husband and wife found it something of a relief when the holiday came to an end, and they returned to Forest Lodge.

As the weeks passed on, the shadow of a new anxiety fell upon Candida. It became only too evident that her mother-in-law was seriously pressed for money. Ominous-looking blue envelopes arrived by nearly every post; the voices of protesting tradesmen were heard from time to time in the hall, and the meals were more than ever insufficient. The new nursemaid complained bitterly of the fare provided, and Candida, who herself was nearly always hungry, was no longer able to supplement the housekeeping out of her allowance. She kept silence as long as she could; but when at last Roley began to look pale and peaked, she felt that it was time to come to an understanding with her mother-in-law on the subject of the household arrangements.

Her opportunity came one afternoon towards the middle of June, when, the drawing-room door having been left ajar, she involuntarily overheard an angry monologue in the hall.

"I don't give no more credit till my bill is settled, or something considerable paid on account," she heard a coarse masculine voice proclaim. "I don't hold with people calling theirselves ladies ordering in the best joints regardless, and then keeping honest tradesmen out of their money. I've waited till I'm tired of waiting; and now I send in no more meat till my account is settled. And if that ain't done pretty soon, I'll take the matter into the county court."

There was a good deal more to the same effect; then the hall-door banged, and a moment afterwards Mrs. Sylvester came into the drawing-room, her face looking white and haggard, her thin hands trembling visibly. Candida felt that to ignore the family skeleton any longer would only be false delicacy.

"I'm afraid you are a little troubled about—about money," she said gently. Does Adrian know? Can't he be of some assistance?"

"No, no; it's only a little temporary embarrassment," stammered her mother-in-law, flushing painfully. "I do not like to trouble Adrian about it; he has anxieties enough of his own just now."

"But I think he ought to know," said Candida. "I hope we are not the cause of any of your difficulties. When Roley was born, I asked Adrian to arrange about the extra expense with you, and he said that he had made it all right; but perhaps you and he may have under-estimated matters. I know that I have been an expensive person to keep during the last few months."

"Oh, my dear, I'm sure you have been most good and patient," answered Mrs. Sylvester, twisting her fingers together nervously. "I know you can't have had enough to eat, and the dear baby is beginning to suffer. If it were not for that, I wouldn't say a word. But I'm afraid it can't go on like this any longer, for the tradespeople won't give any more credit, and we must live. If we could only hold on for a few months, no doubt it would come all right; but, meanwhile, the money is locked up, and I can't get at it."

Candida began to wonder whether her mother-in-law had been indulging in a little private speculation, and was afraid to confide in her son.

"If Adrian knew that you were pressed for money," she suggested, "he might be able to pay the next quarter in advance."

Mrs. Sylvester looked at her uncertainly.

"You see, my dear," she said, "business is a very confusing thing, and you understand even less about it than I do. Poor Adrian's money is all locked up too, but he will make it all right as soon as the market begins to improve again."

"All locked up?" repeated Candida. "But then, how does he manage to contribute to the household expenses?"

"Oh, he is most particular about that; indeed, I fear that he has been only too generous, but he says that when he has a stroke of luck he wishes his old mother to share in it. I have had the full equivalent, and more; I can show you all the papers."

"Equivalent! Papers! I'm afraid I am very stupid, but I don't understand. Do you mind telling me what Adrian really does contribute as our share of the housekeeping expenses?"

"At the rate of two hundred a year at present. It was a hundred and fifty before the baby came. It's too much really, because I never wanted to make a profit out of you."

The sum seemed a sufficient one, for the housekeeping was carried on on so modest a scale that she doubted whether the whole expenditure amounted to more than two hundred a year. But then, why these difficulties?

"But how does Adrian manage to give you two hundred a year, if his money is all locked up?" she inquired.

"Oh, it's perfectly safe, you know," was the enigmatic reply. "It will soon be doubled, I believe; anyhow, it's all accounted for, every penny of it."

"But where is it?" asked Candida, beginning to feel as if her brain would turn.

"In the company—the Automatic Cork-drawing Company. You see, Adrian had promised to take a certain number of shares, and he very kindly let me have some of them as an equivalent for his contribution towards the housekeeping. Of course, it is a splendid thing to be in, or will be in a very short time. But I shall sell out as soon as I can find a purchaser; I don't really care about a high profit."

Candida felt herself turning cold and rigid. "Do you mean to say," she asked, controlling herself by a strong effort, "that you have been paid nothing in money since we came to live here?"

"Oh dear, yes, nearly up to the time that the company was floated. Then, of course, Adrian required all his ready money, so he very liberally proposed to give me his contribution for a year in advance in the form of shares."

"And have they gone up, or paid any interest since you have had them?"

"Well, no, not as yet. You see, it has been such a dreadful year in the financial world, what with panics and long-continued depression, which, of course, Adrian could not possibly foresee. But when once they begin to move, he is confident that they will increase in value very rapidly. I don't like to ask him for an advance after he has behaved so handsomely, and yet I can't bear to think of you and the baby suffering. I'm sure I don't know what is to be done."

Candida was silent for a moment. A hot flush dyed her cheek, and her eyes sparkled ominously.

"I will go up to town this afternoon, and see if I can catch Adrian before he leaves the office," she said. "He is generally detained late on a Monday. He must raise money somehow to pay his debt to you, for the shares may or may not be worth anything in the future. Meanwhile, you shall be relieved of the burden of baby and me; I will take him down to Branksmead to-morrow for the summer. By the time the winter is here I shall be able to work, and provide for him and myself. We will sponge on you no longer."

Something in her voice struck terror into the old lady's heart.

"You won't misjudge Adrian, or do anything hastily?" she pleaded. "A little holiday will do you good, no doubt, and dear baby too. In a few weeks' time things will have changed for the better, and then you will come back, and we shall all be happy and comfortable as before. Don't talk of anything so dreadful as having to work for yourself and Roley; Adrian would never hear of it."

Candida shivered a little. To her mind the idea of coming back to the old life now that her eyes had been opened was quite intolerable, while the prospect of freedom and independence won by her own work shone out like a vision of bliss.

It was nearly six o'clock before she reached her husband's office. The big building in which it was situated looked nearly deserted, and charwomen were sweeping some of the passages, but there was just a chance that he might still be there. The outer office was empty, but she fancied she could hear a murmur of voices in the inner room. There was no answer to her gentle tap, so she opened the door, but stopped short on the threshold with a little cry of surprise. Two persons, a man and a woman, were standing in front of the fireplace, locked in each other's arms. Evidently they had been too much absorbed to hear her knock, but at the sound of a step on the threshold they sprang guiltily apart. The man was Adrian, but the woman? She had hastily let down a thick veil over her face, and then, turning to the mantlepiece, had leant against it, her head bowed upon her arms in evident shame and terror. The shrinking attitude, the quivering form, and the gasping breath that heralded a burst of anguished weeping, struck pity to the intruder's heart, for this was obviously no hardened sinner, but some frail creature who had been tempted beyond her strength. Acting on a sudden impulse, Candida sprang to the window, and flinging up the sash, leant out.

"Run," she called over her shoulder. "I won't look round. Run."

There was a faint swish of silken skirts, a light patter of high-heeled shoes, and the sound of a closing door. Candida waited for a moment to assure herself that the fugitive had got safely off, and then turned round and faced her husband.

CHAPTER XX.

For a moment the pair stood opposite each other in silence.

"Say what you please to me," observed Adrian, at length. "You cannot show more severity than I deserve. Yet I should like to explain that things are not quite so black as they seem, as you probably think them. I admit that I was temporarily infatuated by that—that lady; you told me once that you could understand and make allowances for such a weakness. Our relations were at first only those of flirtation—a romantic flirtation, I confess; but as matters grew more serious between us, she declared that she felt it her duty to put an end to our friendship, and never to see me again. I begged her to grant me one favour, to come here to say good-bye, that we might be alone together for the last time. She came, and she gave me a farewell kiss: it was the first as well as the last; we were never to meet again. The rest you know. She refused to let me lock the door, and therefore we were found out, whereas a more guilty couple would probably have escaped detection."

"I don't want to hear any more," remarked Candida, coldly. "You don't suppose that I imagined you were true to me all these months, do you? But I take no interest in the details of your love-affairs; in fact, your doings or misdoings have become a matter of the utmost indifference to me. I desire neither love nor faith from a man who has proved himself a heartless swindler."

The last words sent the blood to his face like the flick of a whip.

"Swindler!" he repeated angrily. "What do you mean by that? I may have been weak, may have yielded to temptation, but I have never done anything that was inconsistent with the character of a man of honour, as men understand it."

"I have always understood that a man of honour may break his oath to a woman, and even steal away his friend's wife. Such trifles leave no stain upon the dazzling purity of his character. But I never heard that a man of honour was free to swindle his own mother."

"What are you talking about?" he asked, the colour fading from his face. "Will you please explain yourself?"

"Do you think that women and children can eat worthless shares, you man of honour?" she demanded ironically. "It is often said that women do not understand the rules of honour that govern the conduct of men. That is perfectly true. We neither understand nor practise them, and I hope we never shall."

"I suppose you allude to the fact that I paid my mother for our share of the expenses in scrip instead of in cash," he said, trying to control his face and voice. "That was a private arrangement between her and myself which she entered into entirely of her own free will. If you knew anything about business you would understand that I gave her what I believed to be very good value for the money. I quite expected that the shares would have doubled in value before this, and so they would if the times had not been so abnormally bad. But misfortune scarcely deserves the name of swindling."

Candida laughed contemptuously.

"No, but misfortune is apt to fall upon a speculation of the 'wild cat' order. I have heard business men discussing your cork-drawing company, and know how it is regarded by the financial press. You took advantage of your mother's ignorance and her trust in you, to make her invest the money she so sorely needed in a rotten undertaking. My father would have been another victim if I had not put a spoke in your wheel. Do you know that in consequence of your little private arrangement your mother is being insulted and bullied by the tradespeople every day, that we haven't had enough to eat for weeks, and that your sisters are ashamed to visit their friends because their clothes are so shabby? Oh, it makes my heart burn when I think how you and I and the boy have been living like parasites on those poor women, weighing them down and sucking them dry. And you made me think that we were doing them a favour in going to live with them, we who have nearly broken their backs. However, there's an end of it all now—now that I am free."

"Free!" he repeated.

"Yes, you don't suppose that I'm going to play the part of blood-sucker any longer, do you? We'll not burden your mother another day, my boy and I. Even if you could support me, you would have no right to try and keep me with you. You no longer care for me, and you never cared for the child. You have no claim on us, and we make none on you. I take Roley down to Branksmead to-morrow."

"And what if I refuse to let him go?" asked Adrian, seeking for some means of revenging himself for the smart her words had caused him. "The law gives me full power over him, and none at all to you."

Candida turned on him like a tigress who fears an attempt to rob her of her young.

"I defy you to take him from me," she cried, her hands clenched and her eyes gleaming. "I'll keep him though you and all the lawyers in England were against me. What right have you to him? I have bought him and paid for him. Didn't I bear him and care for him? Haven't I fed him and clothed him? Isn't he a part of myself—my very own flesh and blood? What do I care for the law? I wouldn't give him up if all the judges in England stood in a row and demanded him from me. He is my own, and I keep him."

"I never really thought of taking him from you," put in Adrian, glancing at her with a flicker of admiration in his eyes. "I only meant to remind you that I had some right to him too, but I agree with you that it is a legal rather than a moral right. I dare say you will both be much better without me. I know I've behaved like a blackguard to you; don't imagine that I deny it. But I don't want you to think worse of me than I deserve. Believe me or not as you please, I honestly thought that the company would turn out a good speculation; I mean, I felt convinced that we could very soon clear out at a profit. And I never realized that my mother was so hampered for money; things always seemed pretty comfortable when I was at home, and I thought she was such a good manager that she could tide over this little difficulty until I was able to pay her again. I simply haven't known which way to turn for money. I've been at my wit's end. For the rest, I've nothing to say except that I know you've found me a bad bargain, and I admit that you are within your right to be unforgiving."

Candida was silent for a moment.

"Perhaps I may have judged you too harshly and too hastily," she said. "If so, I beg your pardon. And I have no right to be unforgiving on my own account. I do forgive you fully and freely for any wrong you may have done to myself. It may be that I was to blame for your ceasing to love me so soon. Another woman more skilled in feminine wiles and coquetries might have kept you true to her; I was ignorant of all such arts. But now, before we part, let me beg you, if you have still a shadow of regard for me, or any memory of the days when we were all in all to each other, to grant me one last request. Raise money, no matter how, and put an end to the difficulties and anxieties that are slowly killing your mother. I have some necklaces, bracelets, and other trumpery that might fetch a little money; I will leave them behind if you will dispose of them for her. Good-bye. I need not ask you to remain in town to-night. By midday to-morrow I shall be gone."

"Good-bye," he answered reluctantly. "I will get the money somehow, without selling your jewels, I hope. You are quite right to leave me; I have brought you nothing but trouble and disappointment. Well, I hope you will be happy and prosperous now that you are rid of me, you and the boy too."

His voice shook, and his hand trembled as he clasped hers for the last time, for his facile nature was easily moved to emotion, and he felt a keen self-pity as well as some faint idea of the value of the love he had thrown away, as Candida passed slowly from the room. Alone! deserted by his wife, robbed of his child, neither Benedick nor bachelor—it seemed a cruel fate, even though he might be said to have brought it on himself. His fine eyes grew dim as he stood gazing into the empty fireplace, and wondered how such a well-meaning fellow as himself had managed to make such a mess of his life.

* * * * * *

Twenty-four hours later, Candida, with Roley on her knee, was being driven through the shady lanes that lay between the station and her home. She was inclined to condemn herself for the buoyancy of her spirits and the exquisite sense of freedom that filled her heart. But it was impossible to be gloomy or downcast in view of the fact that she belonged to herself once again, that the time of her bondage, first to passion and afterwards to wifely duty, was over, as she believed, for ever.

Her father and mother received her with anxious, mystified faces, for her letter and telegram had told little except that she was coming for a long visit.

"Please don't look so serious," she said, as they sat together under the trees. "I have eloped with Roley, as you see, but I can't tell you all the circumstances that led to the rash act. A difficulty about money was the chief reason that made me leave home, for I am not going back again. Adrian has been unfortunate in business, and we have agreed to part."

"But this is only a temporary arrangement, I hope," said her mother. "When Adrian's affairs improve you will go back to him. A wife's place is beneath her husband's roof."

"He has never given me a roof. No, this is a permanent arrangement. I have other reasons for taking this step which I cannot tell you. I made a mistake in thinking that I could make Adrian happy, that he really needed me. Father, you have a perfect right to say 'I told you so.'"

"I will forego that privilege for the present," he replied. "Indeed, I scarcely feel that I have the right when I see how well and cheerful you are looking. You may have suffered shipwreck, but I expect that you have already set about building a raft."

"Yes, and I have precious salvage," she said, with a glance at her boy, who was sitting contentedly on his grandmother's knee. "Thanks to your unconventional ideas, father, I'm still afloat. If it hadn't been for the opportunities you gave me, baby and I would have been floundering in the water, and deep water too."

"You intend to return to your former profession?" asked Mr. St. John.

"Yes. Miss Mason told me when I left that she had no doubt of being able to find me an opening should I ever desire to take up my work again, and I have already written to her to tell her of my changed prospects. We shall be very glad to stay here during the summer months, Roley and I, but when the autumn comes we must go out into the world again, and begin our work."

Two or three days later Candida came running out to her father, who was working in the garden, with an open letter in her hand.

"Read that," she cried triumphantly. "My raft is built, the sail is rigged, and the flag is flying."

The letter was from Miss Mason, and contained an offer of the post of head instructor of a branch gymnasium which was to be established at Westminster under the same management as that at Bloomsbury. The salary would begin at a hundred and fifty a year, with a percentage on the net profits.

"Well, that sounds promising," said Mr. St. John, when he had read the letter. "I suppose it is the best thing that could happen to you under the circumstances."

"Of course it is. I have the chance of making a fresh start, and beginning life over again. That is better luck than falls to the lot of most people who have made a big mistake."

"Beginning life over again? Yes; but with a weight chained to your leg."

"A weight? Do you mean Roley?"

"No; I was thinking of your marriage vow, which condemns you, a young, healthy woman, to lead a single life."

"I've had quite enough of marriage, thank you," said Candida. "I shall be perfectly contented with platonic relations in the future."

"Ah, you think that now because you have had an unfortunate experience. But men are not all alike, and in time your wounds will heal. It troubles me to think of your anomalous position—neither maid, wife, nor widow."

"No, but woman, mother, worker. Isn't that position definite enough? Ah, here comes Roley with his new playmates."

The boy was carried out by old Lester's daughter Margaret, who had been promoted to the office of nurse. He was laughing and crowing with delight at the antics of some setter puppies that were leaping up and trying to lick his face.

"Isn't he a jolly fellow?" said Candida, laying him on the grass, and letting him roll about with the puppies. "Look, he's not a bit afraid of the dogs. He has got quite sunburnt already from being out of doors so much the last few days. You really must weigh and measure him again, father."

Mr. St. John looked at her, instead of at the baby.

"I haven't yet said, 'I told you so,'" he remarked irrelevantly. "You don't give me the opportunity. You look happier and handsomer than you ever did in your life before. I don't believe you repent not having taken my advice."

"No, I don't. How can I? I have gained so much

more than I have lost. First, there's Roley, and then there's the experience, to say nothing of most valuable lessons in keeping my temper and holding my tongue."

"Ah, but you might have had all those and a good husband to boot, as husbands go. However, if you are satisfied, it is not for me to complain. Have you had any communication with Forest Lodge since you left?"

"Yes," replied Candida, her face clouding over. "I have heard from Mrs. Sylvester and the girls. They think it dreadfully wicked of me to leave my husband, and are scandalized at the idea of my working for a living. They seem to fancy that it will cast a stigma on him. Poor things, I'm very sorry; but if they knew all, I'm sure they would think that I had taken the best—the only possible course."

CHAPTER XXI.

With the passing of summer, Candida went back to town, leaving her boy at Branksmead until she could build a new nest for him. A month's steady practice at the Bloomsbury Gymnasium restored to her a good measure of her former strength and skill, so that by the end of October, when the new establishment was opened, she was able to begin her reign with confidence and courage. The three rooms that she and Sabina had occupied being vacant, she hired them temporarily, since they would just contain herself and her belongings. When the scanty furniture, which was all she could afford, had been brought in, and she had settled down to her new existence, she could hardly believe that the past two years, with her marriage and her life at Herne Vale, had not been some strangely vivid dream. If it were not for the little crib that stood beside her bed, she would have fancied herself a girl again, with all her life before her.

The opening of the new Westminster Gymnasium ushered in a prolonged period of hard and responsible work. The organization of the new institution was left entirely in her hands, and all arrangements were submitted to her, while her assistants had to be initiated into her ways, the hours for classes and private pupils fitted in, and a "good connection" gradually built up. But although a busy time, it was also a very happy and satisfying one, so that past troubles were practically forgotten in the joy of successful accomplishment. To rise in the morning to the knowledge that a day filled with the delightful rush of congenial work lay before her; to come home at night honestly tired and gloriously hungry; to spend long evenings in renewing her acquaintance with some of her old studies, rendered more than ever fascinating now by the thought that she was preparing herself to help Roley on his way to knowledge; to have no time for memories or regrets;—all this made up a lot which, in her eyes, was bliss itself compared with the ordinary feminine existence.

A few months rolled away without bringing much change to our heroine's circumstances, except that as order was gradually introduced into her domain, and experiment gave way to system, she was able to devote more time to the claims of friendship and of society. All links with the short period of her married life had been broken off. Her mother-in-law, she knew, had died in the spring, and the two daughters, left with the tiniest of spinster pittances, had gone to live in a cottage in the country, under the wing of some more prosperous relations. Rumours about her husband reached her from time to time. According to the latest, he was in ill-health, had dissolved his partnership, and gone abroad.

Of her oldest friends, the Ferrars, she had seen scarcely anything since her return to town. She could seldom spare the time to take a journey to Hampstead, and Sabina was apparently too full of more important engagements to be able to accept an invitation to tea; so that, without any quarrel or misunderstanding, they had gradually drifted further and further apart. One evening, however, towards the beginning of her second winter in town, Candida, hastening up St. Martin's Lane, on her way home to tea, suddenly found herself face to face with Ted.

"Why, Candida," he cried, with a start of pleasure, "is that really you? What ages it is since we have met! I have often thought of paying you a visit on my own account, only I knew I was not likely to find you at home. And you haven't been to Hampstead for months."

"No, because Sabina is never at home," laughed Candida. "She seems to work quite as hard at society as any of us at our professions. I have often regretted that we have lost touch of each other so completely; but I felt shy of asking her to come and see me, because I fancied she would think it slow. But won't you come together some Sunday—say, next Sunday?"

"I shall be delighted," said Ted. "And I will bring Sabina, if she has no other engagement; but she has blossomed into such a very fashionable lady, that she is almost monopolized by so-called society."

"Tell me about yourself, Ted," said Candida, as he turned and walked beside her. "You are not looking very well. I expect you are overdoing the work."

"I have to work hard," he said curtly, "and play hard too. I don't like to let Sabina go everywhere alone, and she never seems to care to stay quietly at home. Sometimes I think"—he hesitated—"sometimes I'm afraid that she must be unhappy about something. She is so restless, so eager for excitement; it looks almost as though she were afraid to allow herself time to think. Yet I have done my best to make her happy, poor girl. It may be that she is fretting because she has no child."

Candida looked thoughtful.

"It is a pity that married persons so seldom have the courage to tell each other their secret troubles," she said. "Sabina is the sort of creature to have trials and temptations such as would never occur to prosaic, every-day folk like you and me. However, bring her to see me, and I will try to win her confidence again."

When Sunday came, Ted arrived, according to his promise, but alone. He looked so strange and unlike himself that his hostess's words of welcome died away upon her lips.

"You—you haven't brought Sabina," she stammered.

"Sabina has left me," he answered mechanically. "She's gone away."

"Left you!" repeated Candida, aghast. "You don't mean that——"

"I know nothing beyond the fact," he said. "Yesterday—no, I suppose it was the day before—we had a quarrel. I thought she had been indiscreet, had encouraged a man I distrusted, against whom I had warned her. I lost my temper, and said some harsh things to her, and she—you know how sensitive she was—how she never could bear an unkind word. Perhaps she was frightened, or she may have been wounded by my suspicions. Anyway, when I came home last evening I found her gone."

"Did she leave no note or message?"

"Yes, there was a note, begging me not to try and find her, and telling me I should be much happier without her, as she saw I no longer loved her."

"But have you done nothing—taken no steps to find her?"

"I have done all I could. I went to that brute's chambers, and was told that he had just gone abroad. I am afraid there is no doubt that she went with him. I can do no more. I did my best to make her happy, and I failed; the experiment is at an end. I will give her her freedom if she desires it; the man may marry her."

"Oh, poor Sabina!" cried Candida. "I still can't believe that she is really guilty. She may have been foolish and imprudent, and perhaps your anger frightened her, as you say, and drove her away from you. Remember what a nervous, excitable creature she always was. She may be in hiding somewhere at this moment, longing for you and her home, yet without the courage to go back and ask you to forgive her."

"It would be too late," he said sternly. "My patience is at an end. I will give her money should she need it, but she is no longer my wife. She left me of her own free will, and now the door is shut."

Candida looked at him sadly.

"It is such a pity," she said. "I wish I could help you and her too. But I suppose I can do nothing."

"You can let me come and see you sometimes," he said. "We are both lonely souls now, only you have your boy, and I have no one."

"Come as often as you like," said Candida. "Only promise me to think as kindly as you can of Sabina. I hope that all may yet be well between you and her."

He shook his head gloomily, and bade her good-bye.

The following Saturday he came again, to report that, having heard nothing more of his wife, he had determined to put his house into the hands of an agent, and take chambers in or near the Temple. He asked leave to come again the next day; he was miserable alone in his empty house, he said, and he shrank from going into society or to his club. He was so obviously restless and depressed that Candida thought the kindest thing she could do would be to give him a general invitation to come and see her as often as he felt inclined. If she could lead him to resume his youthful habit of discussing with her the books he was reading, and the ideas that were occupying his mind, nothing would serve more effectually to distract his thoughts from the troubles of the present. Then, from time to time, she could put in a word for Sabina, and try to persuade him to renew his efforts to find her.

This plan answered even better than she had expected, and Ted's visits gradually increased in number and length, especially after he had taken up his abode in the Temple, until at last it came to be regarded as a matter of course that he should spend his Sundays and his leisure evenings with his old friend in Blake Street.

"This is quite like old times," he said one night, as he leant back in his chair with a sigh of content after a stimulating argument over the merits of a new drama, which had lately delighted one half of the public, and scandalized the other. "Do you remember our long talks years ago in the fields at Branksmead? There are some books that I can never open to this day without being reminded of the wood or meadow where you and I read or discussed them together.

Every page is illustrated with memory landscapes, or vignettes of you with your eyes sparkling and your hair blowing in the wind. I can remember your ideas and opinions as clearly as if they were printed as marginal annotations to the book. Ah, those were the happiest days I have ever known."

"We were young and foolish then," Candida answered, smiling. "We lived in the present, and the future was one big hope."

Roley, now more than two years old, was a constant source of pleasure and amusement to the deserted husband, who seldom refused the young man's demands to come and play at "gee-gees," the one game of which he never tired.

"Roley comes of a long line of fox-hunting squires," his mother used to say laughingly. "And he doesn't belie his pedigree. The worst of it is that Margaret Lester, being her father's daughter, encourages his taste for horseflesh. She told me with pride the other day that Master Roley had a wonderful eye for the points of a horse, and that he nearly jumps out of his perambulator at the sight of a beast with fine action."

The winter melted into spring, and with the passing of time the pleasant comradeship became only more firmly cemented. The couple made country expeditions together, went on the river together, visited the theatres together, squabbled, chaffed, talked endless "shop," or maintained a companionable silence, in the manner that is only possible between friends of long standing and close intimacy.

The remembrance of the troubled waters through which both had lately passed grew gradually fainter, and life regained its former zest and savour, so that for the moment they were content with the unthinking, unconscious contentment which is the one really enviable condition of human existence.

Unfortunately, such pleasant and peaceful relations are seldom of long continuance between a man and a woman, for though the woman may sometimes know when she is well off, the man usually wants to "go one better." The world, again, is seldom inclined to leave an innocently happy couple in peace; perhaps because it is jealous of the happiness, and therefore wishes to throw doubts upon the innocence. In this case it was the world in the person of Mrs. Spalding, the wife of a member of the Gymnasium Committee of Management, that was the cause of all the mischief.

Mrs. Spalding was a lady whose sole idea of duty consisted of saying and doing things that were unpleasant to other people. Her sense of duty would impel her to inform her friends that their conduct was being made the subject of disagreeable comment, but never led her to repeat a compliment. To her ears came the rumour that Mrs. Sylvester was making herself conspicuous with a young man. The word "conspicuous" in the social sense, has, of course, only one meaning, and that an evil one. Consequently, Mrs. Spalding felt that it was her duty to inform her young friend of the scandal that was busy with her name.

"You see a good deal of that Mr. Ferrars, don't you, dear?" she said in the course of a Sunday afternoon call on Mrs. Sylvester.

Ted had been present when she arrived, but she had sat him out with inflexible determination.

"Yes, I see him nearly every day," answered Candida. "We are very old friends."

Mrs. Spalding shook her head mournfully.

"Ah, friendship is a beautiful thing," she murmured. "What a pity it is that the world is so censorious. It never can be brought to believe in friendship when the friends are young and of different sexes."

"What do you mean?" asked her hostess, bluntly, for there was innuendo in the visitor's tone and look as well as in her words.

"Well, dear, you know how unkind people are, how ready they are to gossip about young women in your position. A wife who is separated from her husband has to be doubly careful if she would escape calumny. And then—Mr. Ferrars' wife having left him—I'm afraid some people think that you are consoling each other. Of course, I don't believe a word of it," she added hastily. "I have every confidence in you, and so has my husband. Still, I thought it was only right you should know what was being said, in order that you might be just a little more careful in the future."

Candida sat looking straight in front of her for a moment, a deep flush standing in her cheeks. Her friendship was spoilt now, tarnished and poisoned by the world's venomous breath; that beautiful friendship which had brought so much comfort and brightness into her life. She realized its full value now for the first time.

"Thank you," she said at length, speaking almost mechanically. "I will remember what you have told me. I will be more careful."

The visitor having accomplished her mission, presently departed. But Candida sat still, with her chin on her hand, lost in thought. What was to happen now? Was she to give up Ted in obedience to the world's mandate? No, that was absurd, impossible. A real true friendship was too precious a thing to be sacrificed just because a few evil-tongued, evil-minded persons chose to chatter. Even as she came to that decision she shivered at the bare thought of the chatter. She was no longer independent of the world, she could no longer face with contemptuous indifference the shafts of the scandal-mongers, for Roley's mother, like Cæsar's wife, should be above suspicion.

A compromise naturally suggested itself. Perhaps she had been injudicious in seeing so much of Ted, since persons as well as actions are apt to become a habit. They must not meet so often in future; once a week, or, better still, once a fortnight, would be quite enough. She would announce her decision to Ted next time he came, and that would certainly be to-morrow. Yes, she really had been rather imprudent, more especially since her capacity for earning a livelihood depended upon the blamelessness of her character. If it were true that the man who had a wife and children had given hostages to fortune, it was no less certain that the woman who became a mother gave hostages to Mrs. Grundy.

The following evening Ted arrived earlier than usual, for he was full of a new literary project that he had undertaken. This was a series of articles for a legal review upon the differences in the laws as they affect the two sexes, and the causes, both historical and psychological, that had led to such differences. In this work he was anxious to have Candida's advice and assistance.

The hour grew late, and still Ted turned over the leaves of his manuscript, quoted acts and clauses, and made notes or emendations in accordance with the suggestions of his companion. Nothing could have been more innocent or less sentimental than their intercourse, in which even a Mrs. Spalding could have found no ground for criticism.

"Well, I suppose I ought to be going," said Ted, at length, getting up with a sigh of regret. "We seem to be always saying good-bye."

"That is because we meet so often," returned Candida, thinking that here was a good opportunity for explaining the change that she was about to make in the manner of their intercourse. "If we only met once a week, we should only say good-bye once a week."

"That fact is quite indisputable," said Ted, laughing. "You might add that if we never met we should never have to say good-bye. But my objection to saying good-bye to you is not strong enough to lead me to renounce your society."

Candida considered for a moment. When it came to the point, she found that it was not so easy to inform Ted of her decision as it had seemed the evening before, and she felt a little nervous as to the way in which he would receive it.

"If you don't mind," she began hesitatingly, "I think it might be as well if we didn't meet quite so often, for the present, at least. Once a fortnight would really be often enough."

Ted turned upon her eyes full of reproachful surprise.

"You are getting tired of me?" he asked sadly. "I have worn out even your patience and kindness? And all the time I thought that we were such good friends, that you really enjoyed our palavers almost as much as I did myself. Well, that only shows what a blind idiot a man can be, how easily he is taken in by a woman. As long as she listens to him kindly, and pretends to enjoy his society, he never notices how often she yawns behind her hand, how bored she is with him and his egoistic chatter."

"Oh, don't talk like that," cried Candida, throwing prudence to the winds, and relapsing into her native frankness. "I never get tired of my friends, and I am sure I shall miss our talks quite as much as you, if not more. It is not on my own account that I have proposed this change, but the fact is that I heard that—that people were talking—were saying that you and I saw too much of each other."

"The old cats!" exclaimed Ted, savagely. "What business is it of theirs? Besides, people always talk about everybody. You don't mean to say that you paid any attention to that cackle?"

"I had to, because Mrs. Spalding spoke to me about it, and her husband is on the committee of management. There is Roley to be thought of, you know."

"Well, what do you intend to do?" he asked grimly. "Send me to the right-about?"

"No, there can be no necessity for that. But for the present we had better not see each other more than once a fortnight or thereabouts, instead of nearly every day."

"How calmly you arrange it all," he said, with a bitter laugh. "Evidently it is no more to you than if you had settled to have fish for dinner once a fortnight instead of every day. I suppose that women cannot feel friendship any more than love in the degree that men do."

"No; but women prefer half a loaf to no bread, while men demand all or nothing."

"I don't think you can accuse me of having demanded all or nothing," returned Ted. "However, if you have determined to reduce my half loaf to an occasional crust, I suppose that I must submit. When do you propose to bestow the next few crumbs upon me?"

"Now, don't be absurd and unreasonable, because that only makes things harder for me. Let us make up our minds to be patient, and wait for the good time when we shall be old enough to do as we like."

"And too old to enjoy doing anything," he answered moodily. "Why can't people live and let live, instead of martyrizing themselves and each other in the name of some ridiculous fetish called society?"

"That fetish may seem ridiculous to a man," said Candida, "but it is powerful enough to ruin a woman. "So good-bye till this day fortnight."

CHAPTER XXII.

THE fortnight passed with leaden footsteps. Candida was surprised, almost alarmed, to find how keenly she missed her companion of the past few months. Roley had been sent to Branksmead for change of air, so that she was doubly alone. Her heart had long since recovered from the wound that had been dealt it, and her healthy nature had recovered its elasticity, while, like most women of strong vitality, she craved for human sympathy and human companionship more ardently than her sisters of slower pulse and colder blood. Mentally and physically she had now reached her prime, and, complete woman as she was, neither her work nor even her boy could wholly fill her mind, nor satisfy the hunger of her heart.

As the time crept slowly by, she found herself continually thinking of Ted, and counting the days to his next visit. In vain she chid herself for this folly—a folly for which she held Mrs. Spalding mainly accountable, since, if that lady had not occasioned this sudden break in their intercourse, it would have flowed serenely on, and she would never have thought of Ted otherwise than as her old friend, almost her brother. Now, she was always wondering what he was doing, whether he was thinking of her, whether he was very dull without her. She had always appreciated his society, but now she became vividly conscious of his good points. How thoughtful and careful he always was of her comfort when they went about together; her conscience smote her as she remembered that she had sometimes laughed at him for his fussiness. How kind he had been to Roley, too; Roley would miss his playfellow sadly when he came back to town. Then, however busy he might be, he was always ready to advise her in her difficulties, and to sympathize with her about her worries. Lastly, he had kept her in touch with the world of men, told what people were saying and thinking, insisted on her keeping herself *au courant* with the literature of the day, carried her off to see the best plays and pictures,—in a word, had prevented her from letting herself go to rust, as a woman is apt to do when she lives alone, and has no intimate men friends.

The night before their next meeting she lay awake for hours, longing for the dawn, and when the day arrived it seemed as long as the whole fortnight that had preceded it. But at length came evensong, and with it Ted. A strange shyness fell upon the friends as they greeted each other once more; it seemed as if some invisible barrier had been raised between them. At first they talked rapidly and nervously upon indifferent topics, but little by little their unnatural fluency deserted them, and presently they relapsed into silence. For a few moments they sat side by side in the dimly lighted room, each thinking, or rather feeling, what could not be put into words. It was Ted who first broke the silence.

"It seems a hundred years since last Sunday week," he observed, speaking for the first time in natural tones.

Candida answered nothing, though her heart beat a quick assent.

"I thought the fortnight would never end," he went on. "I dare say you'll think me very foolish, but last night I couldn't sleep for thinking that I was to see you again so soon, and all to-day I have been feeling as if the evening would never come. I don't suppose you can understand it, because you have your boy, and plenty of friends besides. You are not so dependent on my society as I am on yours. I never realized how much our friendship meant to me until I was suddenly deprived of it. I feel now like a starving man, who can only look forward to a meal every other week. Perhaps it would be kinder to put him out of his misery once and for all."

"He has the remedy in his own hands," she answered, speaking the more coldly for the difficulty that she had in steadying her voice. It seemed so hard that he should be sad and solitary when she would so gladly give him comfort and companionship.

"Then you wouldn't care if there were an end of it all," he answered bitterly, for his ear was not fine enough to detect the quaver in her voice. "No, I don't believe you would. You are as hard and cold and cautious as the rest of your sex. Women only consider what people will say, and what people will think. When it comes to a choice between prudence and—friendship, they don't hesitate to choose prudence. They will throw over their best friends any moment at the world's bidding."

"I know," she said proudly. "Because we can hold our tongues and control our passions, you say that we have no hearts, just as some modern scientists imagine that we feel pain less keenly than men, because we bear it with more fortitude. Well, you shall have the whole truth for once from a woman's lips, but you will have only yourself to thank if my frankness puts an end to our friendship for ever. Listen, then. I, too, have felt as if the past fortnight were a hundred years—a hundred hundred years; I, too, lay awake last night, longing for the dawn; and I, too, thought this day would never pass. I, too, have been lonely and unsatisfied, and hungering for your return. Is that enough for you? Can I feel? Am I still cold and hard and cautious?"

He had sprung to his feet while she was speaking, and now with one step he was at her side.

"You are an angel," he cried. "Bless you for telling me the truth, for not torturing me to satisfy your vanity or your prudishness. Oh, I can never thank you enough for making me so happy as I am to-night."

"How can you say that?" she said, shrinking away from him, "when you know what this means, what it involves."

"Yes, yes," he returned eagerly. "It means that we belong to each other now. No one else has any claim upon us; those that had have forfeited it."

"It means that we must see each other no more. Our friendship is at an end, and love may not take its place. Wait," she added, as she saw the vehement protest in his face. "Have you ever known a man who had been caught cheating at cards?"

"Yes, I suppose I have," he answered in surprise. "What has that got to do with it?"

"You know how he was punished for his offence. You know that he was regarded as an outcast, a pariah, that even his friends and relations fell away from him, as if he were afflicted with some leprous disease. You know that socially he was dead and buried, though his lonely ghost still flitted about the earth, finding no rest, no comfort, no sympathy. And you know that this dreadful death in life might go on for years and years, till he became an old man, and really died at last, still alone, still an outcast, still a shame and reproach to all who were connected with him. You wonder what all this has to do with you and me. Can't you understand? Don't you realize that society treats a woman who rebels against its unwritten laws precisely in the same manner as it treats a man who has been convicted of cheating at cards?"

Ted fell back a step or two, a baffled look in his eyes.

"Damn society!" he muttered. "Would not you and I be enough for each other?"

"For a little while, perhaps. But afterwards, when youth had passed and passion died out, do you think that we shouldn't feel our, or rather my, isolation? And the more you cared for me, the more grieved and angered you would be to see me disgraced and degraded; and not me alone, but perhaps others no less dear to you. You may say that our social laws are cruel and unjust; perhaps they are. But they were made by men for the benefit of men, and therefore it is unreasonable for a man to complain of them."

He made no answer for a few moments.

"Yes, it is all true," he said at length. "I cannot deny it. But still I see no necessity for our parting. I can bear anything but that. I will be reasonable; I will be satisfied with a half-loaf, with an occasional crust. Let me be your friend and comrade still, if I may be no more."

"Impossible," she said. "Friendship and love cannot exist together; the one burns the other up. We are not children, but grown-up man and woman, and you know as well as I that such an arrangement could have but one ending. You may fancy that you are strong enough to keep within the limits of friendship, never to hint at love by word or look, but I don't believe you are, and I know that I am not."

It was the truth, but the truth is not always prudent from a woman to a man. The confession sent the blood racing through the young man's veins, while a triumphant sense of impending victory filled his heart. He came close to her side, and took both her hands in his.

"You have a man's tongue in a woman's mouth," he cried joyfully. "If I were really never to see you again, the memory of those words would sweeten all my life. But I say that we are to meet as often as we please; I will never let you go. As for the world, we'll throw dust in its stupid eyes, and gag its malignant tongue. We have only to be careful, to keep our own counsel. Of course, if the Mrs. Spaldings of society are to be deceived, we must not meet here, or only at long intervals. To-morrow I will set about making other arrangements, and in the evening I will come once more to talk them over with you."

Candida made one last effort to free herself from the net into which she felt she was being drawn, but her powers of resistance seemed to be gradually melting away beneath the magic of her lover's look and voice and clasp.

"It would be so degrading," she murmured. "We should be always acting a lie, living a hole-and-corner life."

"That would be the world's fault for forcing such a course upon us," he answered. "We should be doing no wrong. There is no law, human or divine, against friendship."

Still holding her hands in his, he bent towards her, his purpose plainly visible in his eyes.

"No, no," she pleaded, turning away her head. "Let us keep up the pretence of friendship as long as we can."

"I will never ask anything of you that you are not willing to give to me freely out of love and kindness," he said, instantly releasing her. "Good-bye, dearest friend, till to-morrow."

As soon as the door closed behind him, Candida dropped into a chair, and moaned in bitter humiliation.

"Oh, what a weak fool—what a weak, cowardly fool I am!"

Now that the spell which his presence exercised over her was removed, she could see clearly the folly, the madness, of the secret compact to which she had tacitly agreed. To-morrow she must tell him that she could not carry out her part in it, must make him understand that it was impossible they should continue to play at friendship, with love always smiling behind the mask. But was she strong enough to see him again, to tell him her decision by word of mouth? Would it not be better, safer, to leave a note for him next evening, and refuse him admission henceforward? And yet, would it be fair or kind to cast him off for ever without so much as a good wish or friendly word at parting? Her own suffering she regarded as no more than a just punishment for her blindness long ago, when she had deliberately chosen the false and rejected the true, but he—ought she not to try and soften his disappointment, to alleviate as far as words could do it, the pain that she was about to cause him? But then, if she were to be unable to resist his prayers and entreaties, if her own heart were to play her false once again, there would be nothing but a renewed and even more agonizing struggle in store for both of them.

These *pros* and *cons* occupied her mind through the long hours of the wakeful night, through the leisure intervals of the busy day, and yet when evening came the problem was not yet solved. She expected her visitor to arrive at eight; the clock struck six, seven, half-past seven, and still she had written no note, given no orders to the servant. A ring at the bell made her start violently, and almost stopped the beating of her heart. Could it be Ted half an hour before his time? If so, it was too late to forbid his entrance, for she could hear Martha already at the door. A dull sense of disappointment and foreboding stole over her as the maid brought in a note. The handwriting was so faint and tremulous that at first she failed to recognize it, but a hasty glance at the contents was sufficient to convince her that the question which had been troubling her was solved, and solved for ever.

The note, which was dated from a street in Chelsea, ran as follows :—

"I am dying; but I can't die in peace until I have seen you once more, and asked your forgiveness for a wrong I have done you. Come to me soon, for I cannot tell how much time may be still left to me.

"SABINA."

Candida put the note, together with a few words from herself, into an envelope, and left it with the servant to be given to Mr. Ferrars when he called. Then, hastily putting on her hat and cloak, she set out upon her journey. It was a long drive to the little street out of the King's Road, where, in the second-floor bedroom of a dingy lodging-house she found her friend.

Sabina was lying on a sofa, wrapped in a faded pink dressing-gown, and looked but the wreck of her former self. Her once brilliant colouring was changed to a waxy pallor, her curly hair cut short, her eyes dull and sunken, and her face so thin that the bones of her cheeks were plainly discernible.

"It was very good of you to come so soon," she said feebly, as Candida entered. "But I thought you would. Please come and sit down close beside me, because my voice is weak. I have so much to tell you, and I am longing to get it over. Then I can die in peace."

"But you——" said Candida. "I am so sorry to see you like this. Why did you come to this dreadful place? Why didn't you let your friends know that you were alone and ill?"

"I'll tell you all about that afterwards, if you still care to hear it. There is something that I must get off my mind first. You won't be very angry with me, will you? You'll promise to forgive me, as I'm dying."

"Yes, yes, of course, though I hope you are not so ill as you think," answered Candida. "I have no right to judge you or anybody else."

Sabina was silent for a moment. Then, turning away her head, she said in a low voice—

"I was the woman you told to run."

For an instant Candida stared at her uncomprehendingly. Then in a flash the half-forgotten scene returned to her mind. The quivering shoulders of a shame-stricken woman, a man standing by pale and defiant, the sight of the grimy court as she leaned out of the window, the sound of rustling skirts and pattering feet.

"You—you were that woman?" she stammered.

"Yes, but don't—please don't be angry with me. It wasn't so bad as you think, though it was bad enough. It all began that summer at Branksmead when I was staying at the Vicarage. I thought it was only fun at first; we were just playfellows, nothing more. But when we went back to town he got into the way of coming to see me, and nearly always when Ted was out, or on circuit. Then, after your baby was born, I came to stay with you, and it was about that time that I first began to get frightened. He was different, and I—you know how weak I have always been."

She stopped to cough, and Candida mechanically pulled up the cushions, and placed her in a more comfortable position.

"Then I came to you at the cottage," went on Sabina. "And you remember that I went home suddenly before the time was up; that was because I dared not stay any longer. Oh, I did struggle, Candida; I thought of you and Ted, and I fought against the temptation with all my might, though I was miserable, and saw that he was too—Adrian, I mean. At last I begged him, for all our sakes, not to come and see me any more, but to keep away and forget me, and allow me to forget him too. In the end, he said he would agree to all I wished, if I would give him one farewell interview at the office, where we should be alone and undisturbed. He said it was his last request, and that after that I should never see him again unless I desired it. I would have consented to almost any condition that would put an end to the struggle; so I went, and we were just taking our last leave of each other when you came in. That is the whole story; I swear it."

"I believe your word," said Candida. "He told me very much the same."

"And can you ever forgive me?"

"Yes, indeed; I stand as much in need of forgiveness as you. I, too, have been weak—only saved by accident, perhaps, from worse than weakness. I know what it is to struggle, and be beaten. But tell me what happened afterwards. Why did you leave your home?"

"I don't know whether I can make you understand. I was so restless and miserable after that dreadful day that I felt sometimes as if I were going out of my mind. It was so lonely, too, and Ted had left off caring for me; I knew he had, though he tried not to show it. When I heard that you had left your husband, I thought that perhaps it was my fault, and I could have killed myself for my treachery. It was about that time that I met old Kesterton, who used to be at the Piccadilly, and he told me that he was going to take out a company to South America, and asked if I would like an engagement. He only meant it in fun, of course, and I thought no more of it till a day or two later. I had a quarrel with Ted about some stupid man or other, and he said dreadful things to me; they hurt me like blows. I knew he would be happier without me, and I was pining for change and excitement—anything to make me forget; so I went off to Kesterton, and told him I had quarrelled with my husband, and would be glad of an engagement. As it happened, some girl had dropped off at the last moment, so he said I could have the vacant place. We sailed two days later, and oh, we had such an awful time!"

"That was how you got ill?" asked Candida.

"Yes, we had to rough it horribly, and I had fever several times. Then I got a chill on the top of that, and had bronchitis. I was in a hospital for weeks at Buenos Ayres, and when I got a little better, they said I had better come home, as the voyage would do me good. But we had such stormy weather that it made me worse, and now I have only come home to die."

"Oh, I hope that is only your fancy. I expect you want nothing but good food and good nursing, such as you can't possibly get here."

"No, it's not my fancy," said Sabina. "The doctor told me I shouldn't recover; at least, he wouldn't say I should when I asked him about it, and he wanted to know if I had any relations I should like to communicate with. Then I understood that it was all up with me. And the landlady says that I have death in my face, and that I look just like her sister-in-law's cousin before she was carried off by a galloping consumption."

"We must get you out of this place at once," said Candida, who had been thinking busily. "There is a room vacant in the house where I am living, and to-morrow I shall bring a carriage and fetch you home. I must have you under my own eye if I am to pull you through, as I hope to do."

"But the money," faltered Sabina. "I have very little, only just enough to see me underground. That is why I came to this place. I couldn't be a burden upon—upon anybody I had behaved ill to."

"I ask you to come as a favour to myself," said Candida, earnestly. "Your presence in the house will be a safeguard to me. Come for my sake, Sabina; you can pay me back some day if you really wish it."

"In the next world," said Sabina, with a dreary smile. "Well, it can't be for long, and I have some jewellery still, which you can have when I am dead. I can't believe in the fable of my presence being a safeguard to anybody, least of all to you."

CHAPTER XXIII.

THE removal was successfully accomplished, and the invalid established in a room adjoining Candida's sitting-room. Here she lay on her sofa from morning till night, languidly awaiting the summons of death. The new doctor who had been called in gave no definite hope of her recovery. She was in a state of extreme exhaustion, he said, and one lung was affected, but the worst symptom of all was her total lack of desire to live. She seemed to be gradually fading away, not so much from any positive disease as from the fact that she had made up her mind to die.

Candida had seen nothing more of Ted, but she had received a short, coldly-worded letter from him, requesting her to do everything that was necessary for Sabina's welfare, and to hold him responsible for all expense that she might incur upon that account. Apparently he had no desire for an interview with his truant wife, nor did he express any interest in her fate. Sabina asked once or twice where Ted was living, and wondered whether he had forgiven her, but she evidently had not the courage to beg that she might see him once more, and receive his pardon from his own lips. Once she expressed her regret that her presence in the house prevented him from enjoying the society of his old comrade.

"You said Ted used to come here sometimes when you were alone," she observed. "It is a pity that you should never see each other now. He never really liked me half as well as he did you; I was only a *pis aller*. I sometimes think," she added, with a little laugh, "that on our wedding-day we—we must have sorted ourselves wrong."

"What do you mean?" asked Candida, feeling ready to kill herself for the blush that she knew had risen to her cheek.

"I mean that in the flurry of the moment we somehow got mixed. I ought to have had Adrian, because I should have understood him, and known how to manage him. I should have teased and coaxed and piqued and provoked him, so that he would never have felt sure of me, and no other woman would have seemed half so interesting. I know exactly how to win and keep that sort of man. Then, of course, you and Ted would have fitted each other like hand and glove. He wanted no managing, and he would have been perfectly happy with a woman who could talk to him and enter into his interests, and he would have asked nothing better than that she should be always the same. He would never have tired either of her or the domestic hearth, while a son would have filled his cup to overflowing. Yes, we certainly sorted ourselves wrong; there are unlooked-for dangers in a double ceremony. However, Ted will soon have a chance of retrieving his blunder. You must be friends with him again when I am gone."

"But I am not going to let you go," said Candida. "If you would only make up your mind to get well, you would soon be about again."

"Why should I? Nobody wants me, nobody cares about me. I have grown such a fright now, and I never had anything to recommend me but my looks. I am much better out of the way."

It was this conversation which put it into Candida's head to try the effect of a new treatment. She wrote to Ted, asking him to give her an interview the next afternoon at the Gymnasium, as she wanted to consult with him about a question that concerned Sabina. Punctually at the appointed hour he arrived, but her heart sank as she looked into his face; its expression was cold and stern.

"Sabina is very ill," she told him. "She gets no better, and unless we can do something to induce her to take some interest in life, I am afraid we shall lose her."

"I am sorry," he said, looking quite unmoved. "Anything in my power——"

"There is one thing in your power that would give her a little comfort—forgiveness. She feels that she has sinned beyond all hope of pardon, and become an object of indifference, if not contempt, to those who once loved her. And Sabina cannot live without kindness, any more than a flower without sunshine."

"What do you want me to do?" he asked. "You can tell her that I am willing to forgive her, if you think that will do her any good."

"I want you to tell her so yourself, to make her understand that she still has a friend in you, that she is not entirely alone in the world, despised of all men. Surely we have no right to say that any wrong is unpardonable, no right to refuse a fellow-sinner a second chance. I only ask you to hold out your hand to her, and help her on her feet again. I want you to give her a little hope, because it is the lack of hope that is killing her more surely than any disease."

"I can forgive her, but I can do no more," he returned. "She treated me with wanton selfishness and cruelty. She has no further claim upon me."

"She makes none, nor I for her, though perhaps if you understood more you would not feel so bitter against her. But, of course, she dared not tell you her secret trials and sorrows, nor ask for pity and consideration in her darkest hour. Sabina was not so heartless as you thought; she was only half distracted with misery, and fighting for something more than life."

"What do you mean?" he asked, turning sharply upon her.

"She thought you had ceased to care for her, and another man came by and filled her empty heart. For the moment she was almost carried away by her infatuation, yet she remembered her duty to you and to others, and she fought against him and against her own heart. Finally she conquered, and they parted. It was then that she tried to deaden her pain, and find forgetfulness in gaiety and excitement. Then came the quarrel, and she fancied that you would gladly be rid of her, so she fled—alone. The rest you know. Oh, Ted, we who have known the misery and fever of forbidden love, we who have so nearly sinned against truth and honour, what right have we to be hard on this poor creature who has been punished so cruelly for all her weakness?

The memory of their last meeting was vividly present with them both. The lines of Ted's face relaxed at last, as he answered more gently—

"No, God knows I have no right to be hard upon her. I will come and tell her that I bear her no ill will, and that she must always look upon me as a friend. Poor girl, I used to fancy she was unhappy, but, of course, I was too stupid to discover the cause."

His voice and manner were warmer than his words, and Candida was satisfied with the result of her interview.

Ted lost no time in carrying out his promise, for he arrived in Blake Street the next afternoon, and asked to see his wife. The invalid was lying on a sofa, a wisp of lace over her hair, and a table by her side, on which stood a vase containing three lilies, and a small Church-service with a very large cross. These were the correct "properties" for a dying girl, and Sabina, though perfectly sincere in her belief in her approaching dissolution, could still feel an artistic pleasure in an effective pose. Ted's heart softened at the sight of her little pale face and unnaturally big eyes. For the first time he felt convinced that her days were numbered; it was so impossible to doubt the evidence of the vase of lilies and the Church-service.

"It is so good of you to come!" she murmured. "I have been hoping to see you once more—for the last time."

"Oh, you mustn't talk like that, you know," he said awkwardly. "I expect you'll soon be better now that Candida has taken you in hand."

She smiled and gently shook her head.

"You are going to forgive me?" she said. "I know I don't deserve it, but it is the last thing I shall ever ask of you. I was selfish and heartless, and you were always so kind and patient. I hope you'll be rewarded for it some day."

"I didn't do anything," he answered gruffly. "I don't think we quite understood each other, but I dare say that was as much my fault as yours. Anyway, I bear no malice, and I'm sure you don't."

"Ah, but the cases are different," sighed Sabina. "You had been so good and generous. Not one man in a million would have behaved as you did after —after all that had happened. I ought to have repaid you with the devotion of my whole life."

"No, by heaven, I can't let you think that," cried Ted. "I had no more right than another man to pose as a superior being, a sort of moral King Cophetua. I married you because I loved you, and if there was any *mésalliance* at all, it was on your side, not on mine."

At this point, greatly to his consternation, Sabina melted into tears.

"And now nobody loves me," she sobbed. "I am ugly and hateful, and a burden on those I have behaved ill to. Why can't I die, and put an end to it all?"

"For God's sake, don't cry like that," exclaimed Ted, anxiously, for tears were to him an alarming mystery. "You'll only make yourself worse, and there's nothing whatever to cry about. I expect I was a stupid clumsy brute; I hadn't the least idea how to treat a woman like you. I dare say it was all my fault. I'm sure I'm very sorry. Sabina, do please stop crying, and say you forgive me."

It was altogether a most unexpected turning of the tables, and Ted could never remember afterwards how he came to be on his knees to his wife, pleading for pardon.

"Of course I do," answered Sabina, through her tears. "I was never hard upon you, was I, Ted? and I never nagged at you as a better woman might have done. And I always made you comfortable, didn't I, and gave you good dinners?"

"You did—you always did," he confessed penitently. "I'm sure I don't know how it was that things went wrong; we were awfully happy at first, do you remember?"

"Yes, weren't we?" returned Sabina. "Ah, one never knows how to value a thing until one has thrown it away. However, everything is forgiven and forgotten now, isn't it, and I can die in peace? And when I'm gone, if we are allowed to watch over those we loved on earth——"

"Oh, don't talk like that," put in Ted, feeling as though the invalid might develop wings before his very eyes. "You'd get well fast enough if you would only try."

"But I don't want to try," she said, the tears still trickling down her pale cheeks. "There's nothing to live for; nobody wants me. And the time seems so long lying here alone all day when Candida is out. I wish you would lend me some books, Ted. Not novels, of course, and nothing very difficult, because my head is so weak. Poetry would be best, I think—serious poetry, you know."

"Yes, yes; I'll bring you some to-morrow," he answered, hastily running over the contents of his bookshelves in his mind. "And perhaps you'd like me to read aloud to you sometimes; it would be better for your head than reading to yourself."

Ted read aloud very well, and knew it.

"Oh, if you only would!" cried Sabina. "I should be so grateful, and I'm sure you will be rewarded for all your goodness some day. Perhaps, when I am no longer here——"

But at this Ted jumped up, and declared that he must not stop any longer, or he would tire her out.

"I'll look in again to-morrow about tea-time," he said, "and bring the books. And I dare say you would like some more flowers," he added, with a respectful glance at the vase of lilies.

It was from the date of this interview that Sabina's health began to improve, and though she still talked about dying, she was soon in a fair way to complete recovery. During her period of convalescence, Ted came nearly every afternoon, generally with a book under his arm, and an offering of flowers in his hand. He began his course of reading with extracts from "Paradise Lost," Young's "Night Thoughts," and the "Christian Year." As Sabina grew stronger, he administered Cowper, then Wordsworth, and finally celebrated the doctor's announcement that there was no more cause for anxiety with a prolonged dose of Burns.

Then August came, and the house at Hampstead, which had been let for the season, was thrown upon its owner's hands again. It was about this time that Ted came to the conclusion that it was rather absurd for a man to have a furnished house in one part of London, and a wife in another, while he himself occupied solitary chambers in a third. Being a young man of sound common sense, with a tendency, rare among mortals, to want what he could have when quite convinced that he could not have what he wanted, he suggested that he and Sabina should give each other another trial, and see whether, with the experience both had gained, they could not make something better out of marriage than a failure. It was finally arranged that, as Sabina's chest was still delicate, they should go abroad for a long holiday, and on their return settle down together in the house at Hampstead.

CHAPTER XXIV.

On a Sunday afternoon, nearly a year later, Candida set out from the little flat in Kensington, to which she had lately removed her small household, to pay a visit to the Ferrars's at Hampstead. It was no ordinary friendly call, however, being nothing less than a visit of congratulation to her friends upon the birth of a daughter. The Ferrars had been at Bournemouth when the event took place, and had only just returned to town, so that this was Mrs. Sylvester's first opportunity of paying her respects to her future god-daughter.

The Ferrars' second venture in matrimonial waters had turned out, in the opinion of the world at least, an unqualified success. The severe discipline that she had undergone had taught Sabina the value of a good husband and a comfortable home, and she rewarded Ted for his kindness with the undiscriminating admiration and spaniel-like devotion so dear to the heart of man. Her delicate health had rendered her indifferent to the charms of society, and she was perfectly content to sit by her own fireside, stitching at some piece of fancy-work, while her husband talked or read aloud. Her quick superficial intelligence caught up with amazing dexterity the more striking of his ideas and opinions, which, slightly coloured and remodelled, she would reproduce in the course of conversation, immensely to his surprise and gratification. So entirely had her personality become absorbed in his, so faithfully did she echo and reflect his thoughts, that he naturally came to regard her as an exceptionally intelligent woman, and wondered that he could have been so blind as to underrate her powers in the past.

The birth of a child had made Ted's cup of happiness run over, and ensured him against disillusionment with his domestic lot in the future. He was one of those men, not uncommon among Teutonic races, in whom the paternal instinct is highly developed, leading them to transfer their passionate devotion from wife to child, while retaining for the former a mild and tranquil affection, mingled with ardent gratitude for the precious gift she has bestowed upon them.

Candida was shown into Sabina's own little sanctum, where the young mother, in the most becoming of tea-gowns, was lying on the sofa, and her husband, seated on a low chair at her side, was gazing at her with the rapt expression of a devotee worshipping at the shrine of a Madonna. It occurred to the visitor that Sabina really did look rather like a Madonna. Her fluffy hair was smoothed down upon her temples, her eyelids were drooped, and her once impudent, up-to-date beauty had taken quite a meek and lowly cast. Candida could not be sure how much of this altered appearance was due to nature, and how much to Sabina's innate sense of the fitness of things.

"You'll like to see Honora at once," said Ted, importantly, as soon as the first greetings had been got over. "We are going to call her Honora, after my mother. I'll go and see if she is awake; she was some time going off to sleep this afternoon, so that she may be later than usual; but I'll tell nurse to bring her as soon as she wakes."

He left the room, shaking the floor with his efforts to attain a noiseless tread.

"Ted is quite beside himself with delight at having a daughter," remarked Sabina, languidly. "He fusses over her like an old hen with one chick."

"And you are pleased too, I hope?" said Candida, struggling to repress the thought that Sabina had grown rather uninteresting since she became a reformed character.

"Oh yes, of course; I shall always have something to occupy me now. And I shall never be afraid of Ted finding out that I am an intellectual fraud, and getting tired of me. The baby's mother will always be sacred in his eyes."

At this point the door was flung wide open, and Ted pranced in again.

"She's awake—she's being dressed—she'll be here directly!" he cried excitedly. "Ah, here she comes!"—as the nurse carried in a bundle of white embroidery. "Now, what do you think of her? Not regularly pretty, perhaps, but a very intelligent expression, hasn't she? and wonderful cranial development. Look, she yawns just like a human being—I mean a grown-up person. Oh, do you think you had better take her, Candida? Are you sure you won't drop her?"

"My dear boy," retorted Candida, "you seem to forget that I was a parent long before you were. Come, Honora, let me feel your muscle. I already look upon her as a future pupil."

The rest of the visit was taken up with baby-talk and baby-worship. When Candida left the house an hour later, she remembered with a gleam of amusement, not unmixed with melancholy, that the fond parents had not asked her a single question about herself, had shown not the slightest interest in her doings, and had not even mentioned Roley, except for the casual remark that in time to come he would make a capital play-fellow for Honora. Ted did not accompany her to the omnibus, as usual, but parted from her on the doorstep, in order to hasten back to his idol, and Candida went on her way alone.

Alone! She felt a wistful pain at her heart as she compared her own lot with that of the couple she had just left, as she remembered their absorption in each other and their child, their complete independence of the world outside. She still had Roley, it was true, but for long? In a few years' time he would go to school, and she knew that the first lesson a British boy learns at school, and the only one he learns thoroughly, is to despise his womenkind. She was aware that the day was not far distant when he would wriggle impatiently from her kiss, and bitterly resent all expression of maternal anxiety and solicitude. Such, her observation had taught her, was a mother's usual reward for bringing a man-child into the world.

She left the omnibus in the Bayswater Road, and walked home through Kensington Gardens. The beauty of the evening, the mellow light, the radiant freshness of the newly awakened trees and flowers, roused in her that yearning to be in harmony with the renewed life of Nature that is only experienced by those who have lost their youth, or in whose ears the world's music rings harshly and out of tune. Candida was still young, not yet six-and-twenty, her natural vigour was unabated, and the blood was still warm in her veins. Her heart had inmates that were cherished with all possible love and constancy, but yet there was room. It was not enough for her to love and serve those who loved her and were themselves lovable, not enough for her to do good work that was pleasant and well-rewarded. There were moments when the "world-sorrow" lay like a dead weight upon her spirit, moments when she longed to gather the whole of suffering humanity into her arms, and hush its cries upon her breast. She could have been happy leading a forlorn hope, championing a losing cause, or heading a crusade against cruelty and oppression, since woman is by nature a fighting animal as long as she knows herself to be on the weaker side, with long odds against her.

Turning into one of the sidewalks, she saw a bath-chair being drawn slowly towards her. Before it reached her the chairman stopped, pulled the chair to the side of the path, and then retired to a little distance to rest and chat with one of the park-keepers. The occupant of the chair, a shrunken-looking man, with a short, grizzled beard, sat perfectly motionless, gazing straight in front of him. Candida was moved by the sight of his forlorn and apparently helpless condition. Had he no mother, sister, or friend, she wondered, to bear him company in his outings? Glancing furtively at him as she came on a level with his chair, she heard him utter her name in timid, uncertain accents, as though he doubted whether she would deign to make any response.

"Candida!"

The voice made her stop abruptly, and turn wide, startled eyes upon the speaker, for it was a once familiar voice, the voice of her husband.

"Adrian!" she gasped, going close up to him,

and gazing into his face. Yes, it was he, changed and worn and prematurely grey, but unmistakably he.

"I don't wonder you didn't recognize me," he said, with a faint smile. "You are not altered except for the better."

"You are—you have been ill?" she said, still scarcely able to collect her thoughts. "Why didn't you let me know?"

"I'm done for," he answered quietly. "You remember how the doctors were always croaking at me, and threatening me with awful consequences if I didn't change my ways. I never paid much attention to them at the time, but the old boys were true prophets for once."

"Do you mind telling me what is the matter?"

"Paralysis," he replied. "They say I may live for years without getting much worse, but I shall never be any better."

"Oh, poor Adrian!"

Her eyes filled with tears as she looked around her, and remembered how he and she had walked together in those gardens in the early days of their love. There were young lovers still wandering hand in hand along the flower-bordered paths, while he—— The trees and shrubs grew dim before her eyes.

"I am so sorry," she faltered, recognizing the utter futility of words. "Is there no hope of cure?"

"No, none. Of course. I've only myself to thank, but I don't know that that makes it any better."

"Will you tell me where you are living? I hope you are comfortable—that you have all you want."

"I've got a room in Golden Ball Street, Notting Hill. It's rather a slummy neighbourhood, but I chose it because it was the cheapest place I could find within easy reach of the Gardens. I lost all my money, as perhaps you heard. An uncle makes me a small allowance, but it doesn't run to luxuries. That fellow over there comes in morning and evening to dress me and put me to bed, and three times a week he takes me out in a chair; I can't afford to have it every day. For the rest, the landlady and her husband and the slavey look after me between them."

"But have you no one to come and see you—no occupation? How can you get through the day?"

"Well, now and then an old pal drops in to play piquet with me, but it's dull for them, of course, so I can't expect them to come often. Then I have the papers—I never cared much about books, you remember—and I draw a little, and sometimes the landlady comes in and talks to me. Oh, I pass the time somehow."

Candida listened to his simple statement with mingled admiration and astonishment. How could he bear his terrible fate with such apparent cheerfulness and resignation?

"I wish you had let me know," she said. "I would so gladly have come, and brought Roley with me. But now—now that I have found you I will try and make things easier for you. I will learn some games, and come and sit with you as often as I can."

"You are very kind and forgiving. I hadn't the cheek to write to you after—after all that had happened, and I've only been back in town a short time. I was in Germany last year, trying the baths, and after that I stayed with the girls. They are still called the 'girls,'" he added with a smile.

At this point the chairman came up and suggested that it was time to be moving homewards.

"May I come with you?" asked Candida; "then I shall know my way another time."

"I shall be delighted," he replied. "And I will give you some tea, or rather you will have to give it to me."

She walked by his side until they reached his lodgings, a tiny ground-floor in a back street. The chairman brought out a crutch, with the help of which, and the man's arm, Adrian was able to drag himself into the house.

"The landlady will bring in the tea as soon as the kettle boils," he said, when he was safely established on the horse-hair couch. "She is a good-natured old body, and often pops in to 'cheer the poor gentleman up a bit.' Unfortunately, the slavey is not amusing, like the slaveys in novels, though she is quite as dirty."

"I can't think how you can bear it," broke in Candida, passionately. "How can you be so patient and cheerful under such an affliction? I should be ready to cut my throat."

"One bears things because one has to, I suppose," he said carelessly. "How nice it is to have tea poured out by a lady again. It makes me feel quite fashionable and elegant. I hope you don't despise water-cresses? My landlady always sends some in because she thinks I must want a relish with my bread and butter. I never could see that there was much relish about water-cresses, but I graze on them every day rather than hurt her feelings."

He chatted on easily and naturally till it grew dark, and Candida began to put on her gloves.

"Will you wash my hands for me before you go?" he asked. "I don't like to ask the slavey to assist at my ablutions too often, because it gives her such a low opinion of my intellect."

Candida silently fetched a basin of water, and held it for him while he washed his hands. A warm raindrop falling into the basin made him look up suddenly.

"You are not crying!" he said in surprise. "Crying over me! Don't do that; I'm not worth it."

She put down the basin, and came and knelt by his side.

"Adrian," she said between her tears—"Adrian, I can't leave you here except for this one night longer.

You must come back to me. To-morrow I will come and fetch you home."

"No, no; you don't know what you are saying," he returned quickly. "You have been shocked and startled by coming upon me unexpectedly. This is one of your Quixotic impulses, but I won't take advantage of you. The best advice I can offer you is to get a divorce. I could give you a technical slap before a witness—the bath-chairman would do—and the other evidence would be forthcoming. I wouldn't defend the case, so there would be very little unpleasantness. Then you could marry a nice young man with straight legs and curly hair, and live happily ever after."

"But I don't want a young man with cur—curly hair," she sobbed. "I only want somebody who wants me, and you *do* want me now, Adrian. I thought you needed me years ago, when I was a foolish girl, blinded by vanity. I fancied I could help you then, but I know I can now, if you will only let me."

"I don't think you realize what you are proposing," he said, turning away his head so that she might not see the longing in his eyes. "Do you understand that I may live, a helpless invalid, for ten, twenty, even thirty years, that I shall never be any better, but that I must in time grow worse, that my brain will probably become affected? Then I am not certain of my allowance. My uncle, who is a mean old hunks, might stop it if he thought you were able to support me."

"That makes no difference," she cried eagerly; "I can manage perfectly. I have saved money, and I can easily make more if I work longer hours. We have a spare-room now, and I will get a properly trained servant to attend upon you. Then you will have me in the evenings, and Roley will be company for you too. He is four years old, you know, and such a dear little fellow; I am sure you would like him now."

He was silent for a moment.

"I remember," he said slowly, "that your father used to say that a liberal education hadn't been able to knock the woman out of you, and I'm sure I don't know why the dickens it should. But this plan is cruel—barbarous to you. I have no claim upon you, remember; I forfeited that long ago. How can I accept your offer, knowing that you will probably repent of it some day?"

"Never, never!" she exclaimed. "How could I ever be happy as long as I knew that you were here alone, neglected and uncared for? I should always see you as I did this afternoon, sitting in your chair, helpless and deserted, yet looking so patient and resigned. It would come between me and everything else—nothing could give me any pleasure as long as that memory was tugging at my heart."

She put her arm round him, and drew his grey head down on her shoulder.

"Now it is all settled," she said in coaxing tones. "You are not to have your own way any more. To-morrow morning I shall come and carry you off home with me."

"How can I refuse?" he muttered helplessly; "how can I refuse? It does seem a howling shame, but you have tempted me beyond my strength."

He leant back among his cushions, and watched her as she moved about, tidying up the room, and making all ready for the night. The teaching of ages had already begun to re-assert its power, and was soon to put an end to his instinctive shrinking from the proposed sacrifice. After all, he reflected, she was his wife, and in the eyes of the world it would be no more than right and fitting that this strong and splendid creature should offer up herself, her youth and her beauty, at the shrine of her disabled husband; that she should bear upon her shoulders the burden of his shattered life, and act as his unpaid nurse and handmaid till death did them part. He began to feel that he was doing her a favour in providing her with such an unparalleled opportunity for the self-immolation that all true women are supposed to love. There was even a faint tinge of patronage in his manner as he bade her good night, and promised to hold himself in readiness on the morrow for his removal to his new abode.

And Candida walked home through the darkening streets, her eyes shining because the future lay dim before her, her step buoyant because the yoke was upon her neck again, her mind at ease because she had just assumed a grave responsibility, and her heart satisfied because she had flung all hopes of happiness away.

THE END.

www.ingramcontent.com/pod-product-compliance
Lightning Source LLC
Chambersburg PA
CBHW032102230426
43672CB00009B/1611